ENCOUNTERING THE HEALING POWER OF GOD

ENCOUNTERING THE HEALING POWER OF GOD

A Study in the Sacred Actions of Worship

Robert E. Webber

The Alleluia! Series of the Institute for Worship Studies

HENDRICKSON PUBLISHERS

Hendrickson Publishers, Inc.
P. O. Box 3473
Peabody, Massachusetts 01961-3473

ENCOUNTERING THE HEALING POWER OF GOD:
A Study in the Sacred Actions of Worship
by Robert E. Webber

ISBN 1-56563-274-5

CONTENTS

Welcome vii

Introduction ix

PART I: SACRED ACTIONS ORDERED BY THE LORD

SESSION 1. Actions Speak
A Study in Sacred Actions 2

SESSION 2. The Symbol of Water
A Study in Baptism 9

SESSION 3. Getting Ready for Baptism
A Study of Baptism in the Early Church 16

SESSION 4. Do This in Remembrance of Me
A Study in the Sacred Actions of the Lord's Table 24

SESSION 5. Thank-You
A Study in the Eucharist of the Early Church 33

PART II: SACRED ACTIONS COMMONLY ACCEPTED BY THE CHURCH

SESSION 6. I Believe
A Study in Confirmation 42

SESSION 7. Forgive Me
A Study in Reconciliation 49

SESSION 8. I Do
A Study in Marriage 57

SESSION 9. Set Apart
A Study in Ministry 64

SESSION 10. Heal Me
A Study in Anointing 72

SESSION 11. Ashes to Ashes
A Study in Funeral Rites 78

PART III: OTHER SACRED ACTIONS OF WORSHIP

SESSION 12. Humble Yourself
A *Study in Foot Washing* 86

SESSION 13. Return to the Lord
A *Study in the Solemn Assembly* 93

WELCOME TO THE ALLELUIA! SERIES

This Bible study series has been designed by the Institute for Worship Studies primarily for laypersons in the church.

We are living in a time when worship has become a distinct priority for the church. For years, the church has emphasized evangelism, teaching, fellowship, missions, and service to society to the neglect of the very source of its power—worship. But in recent years we have witnessed a Spirit-led renewal in the study and practice of worship.

Because worship has been neglected for so many years, there is precious little information and teaching on the subject in our seminaries, Bible schools, and local churches.

The mission of the Institute for Worship Studies is to make the study of worship available to everyone in the church—academician, pastor, worship leader, music minister, and layperson.

Laypersons will find the seven courses of the Alleluia! Series to be inspiring, informative, and life changing. Each course of study is rooted in biblical teaching, draws from the rich historical treasures of the church, and is highly practical and accessible.

The Institute for Worship Studies presents this course, *Encountering the Healing Power of God: A Study in the Sacred Actions of Worship,* as a service to the local church and to its ministry of worship to God. May this study warm your heart, inform your mind, and kindle your spirit. May it inspire and set on fire the worship of the local church. And may this study minister to the church and to the One, Holy, Triune God in whose name it is offered.

THE SEVEN COURSES IN THE ALLELUIA! WORSHIP SERIES

Learning to Worship with All Your Heart: A Study in the Biblical Foundations of Worship

You are led into the rich teachings of worship in both the Old and the New Testaments. Learn the vocabulary of worship, be introduced to theological themes, and study various descriptions of worship. Each lesson inspires you to worship at a deeper level—from the inside out.

Rediscovering the Missing Jewel: A Study of Worship through the Centuries
This stretching course introduces you to the actual worship styles of Christians in other centuries and geographical locations. Study the history of the early, medieval, Reformation, modern, and contemporary periods of worship. Learn from them how your worship today may be enriched, inspired, and renewed. Each lesson introduces you to rich treasures of worship adaptable for contemporary use.

Renew Your Worship! A Study in the Blending of Traditional and Contemporary Worship
This inspiring course leads you into a deeper understanding and experience of your Sunday worship. How does worship bring the congregation into the presence of God, mold the people by the Word, and feed the believers spiritually? The answer to these and other questions will bring a new spiritual depth to your experience of worship.

Enter His Courts with Praise: A Study of the Role of Music and the Arts in Worship
This course introduces you to the powerful way the arts can communicate the mystery of God at work in worship. Music, visual arts, drama, dance, and mime are seen as means through which the gospel challenges the congregation and changes lives.

Rediscovering the Christian Feasts: A Study in the Services of the Christian Year
This stimulating and stretching course helps you experience the traditional church calendar with new eyes. It challenges the secular concept of time and shows how the practice of the Christian year offers an alternative to secularism and shapes the Christian's day-to-day experience of time, using the gospel as its grid.

Encountering the Healing Power of God: A Study in the Sacred Actions of Worship
This course makes a powerful plea for the recovery of those sacred actions that shape the spiritual life. Baptism, Communion, anointing with oil, and other sacred actions are all interpreted with reflection on the death and resurrection of Jesus. These actions shape the believer's spiritual experience into a continual pattern of death to sin and rising to life in the Spirit.

Empowered by the Holy Spirit: A Study in the Ministries of Worship
This course will challenge you to see the relationship between worship and life in the secular world. It empowers the believer in evangelism, spiritual formation, social action, care ministries, and other acts of love and charity.

Take all seven courses and earn a Certificate of Worship Studies (CWS). For more information, call the Institute for Worship Studies at (630) 510-8905.

INTRODUCTION

Encountering the Healing Power of God: A Study in the Sacred Actions of Worship may be used for personal study or a small-group course of study and spiritual formation. It is designed around thirteen easy-to-understand sessions. Each session has a two-part study guide. The first part is an individual study that each person completes privately. The second part is a one-hour interaction and application session that group members complete together (during the week or in an adult Sunday school setting). The first part helps you recall and reflect on what you've read, while the small-group study applies the material to each member's personal life and experience of public worship.

Encountering the Healing Power of God is designed for use by one or more people. When the course is used in a group setting, the person who is designated as the leader simply needs to lead the group through the lesson step by step. It is always best to choose a leader before you begin.

Here are some suggestions for making your group discussions lively and insightful.

SUGGESTIONS FOR THE STUDENT

A few simple guidelines will help you use the study guide most effectively. They can be summarized under three headings: Prepare, Participate, and Apply.

Prepare

1. Answer each question in the study guide, "Part I: Personal Study," thoughtfully and critically.

2. Do all your work prayerfully. Prayer itself is worship. As you increase your knowledge of worship, do so in a spirit of prayerful openness before God.

Participate

1. Don't be afraid to ask questions. Your questions may give voice to the other members in the group. Your courage in speaking out will give others permission to talk and may encourage more stimulating discussion.

2. Don't hesitate to share your personal experiences. Abstract thinking has its place, but personal illustrations will help you and others remember the material more vividly.

3. Be open to others. Listen to the stories that other members tell, and respond to them in a way that does not invalidate their experiences.

Apply

1. Always ask yourself, "How can this apply to worship?"

2. Commit yourself to being a more intentional worshiper. Involve yourself in what is happening around you.

3. Determine your gifts. Ask yourself, "What can I do in worship that will minister to the body of Christ?" Then offer your gifts and talents to worship.

SUGGESTIONS FOR THE LEADER

Like the worship that it advocates, the group study in *Encountering the Healing Power of God* is dialogic in nature. Because this study has been developed around the principles of discussion and sharing, a monologue or lecture approach will not work. The following guidelines will help you encourage discussion, facilitate learning, and implement the practice of worship. Use these guidelines with "Part II: Group Discussion" in each session.

1. Encourage the participants to prepare thoroughly and to bring their Bibles and study guides to each session.

2. Begin each session with prayer. Since worship is a kind of prayer, learning about worship should be a prayerful experience.

3. Discuss each question individually. Ask for several answers and encourage people to react to comments made by others.

4. Use a chalkboard or flip chart or dry-erase board. Draw charts and symbols that visually enhance the ideas being presented. Outline major concepts.

5. Look for practical applications of answers and suggestions that are offered. Try asking questions like, "How would you include this in our worship?" "How would you feel about that change?" "How does this insight help you to be a better worshiper?"

6. Invite concrete personal illustrations. Ask questions like, "Have you experienced that? Where? When? Describe how you felt in that particular situation."

7. When you have concluded Session 13, send the names and addresses of all the students who will complete the class to: Institute for Worship Studies, Box 894, Wheaton, IL 60189. We will then send a certificate of accomplishment for each student in time for you to distribute them during the last class. The cost of each certificate is $1.00. (Add $3.00 for postage and handling.)

One final suggestion: Purchase the larger work upon which this course is based, volume 6 of *The Complete Library of Christian Worship.* This volume, entitled *The Sacred Actions of Christian Worship,* is a beautiful 8½-by-11-inch coffee table book that will inform your mind and inspire your heart through hours of reading and study.

PART I

SACRED

ACTIONS

ORDERED BY

THE LORD

ACTIONS SPEAK

A Study in Sacred Actions

When I was about ten years old, a U.S. Army general came to our town to speak. It was a big occasion in a small town, so the turnout was large. My dad and I went to hear the general and experience the festivities.

After the speech my dad and I were standing in the path of the general's exit. As he passed by us, he patted me on the head and said, "What's your name, sonny?" I was embarrassed and scared, so I lowered my head and mumbled my name.

The general walked on, and my dad used this as an opportunity to teach me how to meet people. "Robert," he said, "when you meet someone, you look him in the eye, you clasp his hand firmly, and you speak clearly and distinctly." On that day I learned that a greeting with a firm handshake and a clear look is an action that speaks.

Of course we all know that. And we all can remember significant handshakes. It is an instant form of communication, an action that speaks.

Life is full of symbolic gestures and words that speak and act. Events like birth, graduation, marriage, and death are attended by ritual actions. We communicate not only through what we say but what we do.

This study is all about actions that we do in worship. We want to know how they speak and how we can hear what they have to say.

THE BIBLICAL BASIS OF SACRED ACTIONS

In Isaiah 6 and Revelation 4 the creatures of God are worshiping. Both Isaiah and John were smitten with the holiness of God and heard creatures around the throne cry, "Holy, holy, holy is the Lord God Almighty, who was, and is, and is to come" (Rev 4:8, cf. Isa 6:3).

A fascinating feature about this vision is the symbolism that surrounds God on the throne. Isaiah sees God "seated on a throne, high and exalted, and the train of his robe filled the temple. Above him were seraphs, each with six wings: With two wings they covered their faces, with two they covered their feet, and with two they were flying" (Isa 6:1–2). John's description is even more elaborate (see Rev 4:6–5).

Why Recover Symbolism in Worship?

We need to recover symbolism in worship because human beings are symbolic creatures. Recent research in psychology, especially the branch that attempts to understand the neural organization of the human brain, has concluded that the brain functions differently in the right and left hemispheres. The left hemisphere appears to specialize in verbal functions, and the right hemisphere centers on spatial functions and other nonverbal skills. While Scripture is verbal, it uses a variety of communication models, ranging from discursive expression to highly apocalyptic language to poetry.

Psychoanalyst Rollo May argues that the loss of symbols constitutes one of humanity's chief difficulties. When people have no symbols to identify and illustrate the meaning of life, they cannot transcend the crises of life. Hunger, war, death, unemployment, disease, and the other horrors that confront civilization on a daily basis seem to be the sum and substance of life. Signs or symbols in this world show people another world, or means of coping with the trials and strains of this world. Without them, people have nowhere to turn but to despair and absurdity.

Furthermore, symbolism is at the very center of life itself. The celebrations that mark such occasions as birthdays, anniversaries, graduations, marriages, and funerals are all ways of *acting out* the meaning of things that words alone fail to convey.

Principles to Guide the Restoration of Symbolism in Our Worship

First, it is necessary to recognize that earthly worship is modeled after a heavenly pattern. The visions of Isaiah and John affirm the use of symbolism in worship. Obviously it is impossible and inadvisable to literally reproduce the elements of their visions. On the other hand, when the earthly church refuses to incorporate visual symbols into its worship, it misses an opportunity to join the heavenly hosts in ascribing worth to God.

Second, it is important to recover worship as an action. It is something we do—not something done to us. The visions given to Isaiah and John indicate that worshipers are not merely passive observers. They are involved in *doing* something. In John's account, the creatures did not rest "day or night," the elders "[fell] down before Him" and "cast their crowns before the throne" (Rev 4:8, 10 NKJV). Worship involves an active response from the worshiper.

In the history of Christian worship there has been a strong emphasis on what the worshiper does. In the Catholic and Orthodox traditions the worshiper genuflects, kneels, sings numerous responses, bows, says "amen" at the end of prayers, walks forward for Communion, smells the incense, hears the bells, sees the Host, and passes the kiss of peace. Charismatic worship is also quite active. Charismatics raise their hands, speak in tongues, interpret, prophesy, sing in the Spirit, and sometimes dance spontaneously. In this sense Catholics, Orthodox, charismatics, and others who stress the involvement of the whole person in worship are using a greater variety of symbolic actions than those who merely sit and expect to be challenged or filled.

Finally, we must always keep in mind that worship is a learned art. The idea that worship is instantaneous, spontaneous, and natural betrays our lack of understanding. We are more than willing to agree that a successful musician, artist, dramatist, doctor, teacher, lawyer, carpenter, or homemaker must learn the art of doing his or her profession right! Yet we somehow feel that the Christian faith, worship, and the communication of Christian truths should all fall into place naturally without any effort on our part. For this reason it is important to emphasize both the *learned* and the *artistic* nature of worship. The process by which it has been learned is historical. The interested reader will want to examine various church liturgies for special holy days such as Christmas, Easter, and Pentecost. Symbolism occurs in the vestments, architecture, and music of the church, and each area provides additional ideas for recovering symbolism in the contemporary church.

CONCLUSION

We have been able to see that symbolism has always played a very important part in Christian worship. Therefore, the great drama expressed in Scripture, from the fall to the restoration of humanity in Jesus Christ, ought to be communicated not only in words but in actions. Symbolic communication in the church is a valid means of communicating truths of the Christian faith. The reenactment of the birth of Christ, the sorrow over his death, the joy of his resurrection, and the power of Pentecost cannot be completely nor adequately communicated through words alone. The same can be said for the other sacred actions that we will study in this course: baptism, the Lord's Supper, anointing with oil, foot washing, and the many other sacred actions of worship require nonverbal means of communication. This study will ask you to pay close attention to these sacred actions that communicate the meaning of the gospel.

STUDY GUIDE

Read Session 1, "Actions Speak,"
before starting the study guide.

PART I: PERSONAL STUDY

Complete the following questions individually.

1. *Life Connection*

◆ Think of a special occasion in your life, your family, your church, or the nation that demanded some form of symbolic communication. Recount that event and the significance of each symbol used.

_____

_____

_____

2. *Content Questions*

◆ Read Revelation 4:1–11. List as many symbols as you can find in the text. What do these symbols communicate? _____

_____

_____

_____

_____

◆ Compare the communication skills of the right and left sides of the brain.
Left_____

_____

Right _____

_____

◆ How does Scripture affirm the use of symbol as well as reason?

_____

_____

_____

_____

◆ Describe psychoanalyst Rollo May's argument for the use of symbolism.

_____

_____

_____

_____

_____

_____

◆ Give an example of symbolism in everyday life.

_____

_____

_____

_____

_____

_____

◆ State and describe in your own words three principles to keep in mind as we consider the nonverbal character of worship.

_____

_____

_____

_____

_____

_____

3. *Application*

◆ Recall a meaningful nonverbal action that spoke to your heart in a recent service of worship. _____

_____

_____

_____

_____

PART II: GROUP DISCUSSION

The following questions are designed for group discussion. Share the insights you gained from your personal study in Part I.

Write out all answers that group members give to the questions on a chalkboard, a flip chart, or a dry erase board.

1. *Life Connection*
- Begin your discussion by recalling incidents from personal life, family life, church life, or national life that required symbolism to communicate meaning.

2. *Thought Questions*
- Read Isaiah 6:1–7 and discuss the meaning of the symbolism.
- Read Acts 2:42–47 (the earliest description of Christian worship) and discuss the symbolic actions that took place in early Christian worship.
- Read Revelation 4:1–11 and discuss the symbolism of heavenly worship.
- Ask for examples that would confirm Rollo May's contention that symbolism is a necessary element of life.
- Discuss the three principles that we need to keep in mind as we use symbolism in worship.

3. *Application*
- Evaluate all the symbols used in a recent worship service in your church. What would worship have been without these symbols?
- Imagine a service that is absolutely void of any form of symbolic communication. What would it be like?
- Discuss how your present worship could be enhanced by the greater use of symbolic communication. What symbolic forms of communication would you add?

THE SYMBOL OF WATER

A Study in Baptism

 I was twelve years old when my dad sat me down and said, "Robert, don't you think it's time for you to be baptized?"

His question gave me the opportunity to give some careful thought to my relationship with Jesus Christ. Did I believe that God was there? Did I believe that God sent Jesus Christ to die for me? Was I willing to make a commitment of life in baptism to this person and to these teachings?

I remember actually pondering these questions and coming to the conclusion that while I didn't know very much about Christian thought, I was willing to make a real commitment.

That was a long time ago. And now, many years later, when someone says to me, "At what point did you become a Christian?" I always answer "I grew up in a Christian home and never rejected the Christian faith. But my first personal conscious embracing of Jesus came at age twelve at my baptism."

I am able to identify my baptism as my personal conscious beginning in the Christian faith because of a powerful symbol that took place during my baptism. As I was standing in the water, my dad (he was the pastor of the church) said to me, "Robert, do you renounce the devil and all his works?" At twelve years of age, I hardly even knew what the works of the devil were. I said, without a full consciousness of what it meant, "I do." In that very moment I was plunged into the water, as in a tomb, to die with Jesus and bring death to my sins. Then I was raised up out of the water to be resurrected with Jesus to a new life!

Let us explain this powerful symbol of initiation into Jesus.

THE BIBLICAL UNDERSTANDING OF WATER BAPTISM

Let's begin our search for a biblical understanding of water baptism by looking at the symbolic meaning of water in the biblical literature.

The two primary Old Testament symbols of water are the flood and the Red Sea. The flood symbolizes a judgment of dissolution and purification (Gen 6:1–9:17). The Red Sea symbolizes a new beginning, a passageway from the old life (in the wilderness) to a new life (in the promised land). The water of the Red Sea is renewing and life giving, not destructive (Exod 14:8–31).

These two themes—water as destroying and water as renewing—are brought together in the baptismal teaching of the New Testament.

While the New Testament is full of baptismal teaching, scholars recognize that the two most significant passages on baptism were written by Paul (Rom 6:3–11) and John (John 3:1–16).

In Romans 6:3–11 the apostle Paul clearly follows the Old Testament tradition that water is both a symbol of destruction and a symbol of new life: "We were," says Paul, "therefore buried with him through baptism into death in order that, just as Christ was raised from the dead through the glory of the Father, we too may live a new life" (v. 4). Because of our baptism into the death of Jesus, our sinful nature is brought to life. Because of our baptism into the resurrection of Jesus, a new nature and a new life has been given.

Jesus clearly teaches this theme of death and resurrection. In his famous dialogue with Nicodemus he likens a relationship to God through a baptism into himself as a new birth: "no one can enter the kingdom of God unless he is born of water and the Spirit" (John 3:5). Jesus is referring here to that powerful symbol of water: death to the old, birth to the new. (Note that water baptism is associated with the gift of the Holy Spirit. See Mark 1:10; Acts 10:38. This matter is discussed in Session 6.)

PREBAPTISMAL INSTRUCTION

The biblical view of water as symbolizing destruction and a new beginning also occurs in the teaching given by the New Testament church to new believers who were preparing for baptism.

Scholars recognize several cases in the New Testament where new believers were baptized immediately. This was certainly true of the Ethiopian eunuch (Acts 8:26–38) and the Philippian jailer (Acts 16:16–40). Many argue the same for Acts 2:38–41, but this is a problematic passage. The phrase "many other words" (v. 40) may mean a lengthened time of teaching. The word *day* in v. 41 may be interpreted as the day of the Lord—the new time since the resurrection—as opposed to a twenty-four-hour day.

The suggestion that there was a lengthened time of teaching before baptism is strengthened by the presence within the New Testament of vestiges of ancient catechesis (instruction). Many believers coming from a pagan background had no knowledge of the Christian way of life. Consequently, it seems likely that when they became believers they were in need of instruction in the Christian way, and spent some time learning about the Christian life before they were baptized and admitted into the full fellowship of the church.

A quick survey of the following passages shows us that they are rooted in the dual theme of the baptism symbol: destruction of the old and birth of the new. Consider the following summary:

Romans 7:15–23	No longer slaves of unrighteousness But slaves of righteousness
Colossians 3:1–17	Put off the old man Put on the new
Galatians 5:13–25	No longer walk after the flesh Walk after the Spirit

CONCLUSION

When we go back to the New Testament and attempt to reconstruct the experience of water baptism, we are struck by the symbol of water as a sign of destruction and a sign of new life. Water kills (as in death to sin) and water brings to life (as in the birth of a new way to life). We need to make more of the powerful symbol of water so that it reminds us of our relationship to Jesus Christ.

STUDY GUIDE

Read Session 2, "The Symbol of Water,"
before starting the study guide.

PART I: PERSONAL STUDY

Complete the following questions individually.

1. *Life Connection*

◆ Take time to recall your baptism. What do you remember most from that experience? If you were baptized as an infant, how do you mine the symbol of baptism for your spiritual life, even though you have no memory of your own baptism? _____

_____

_____

_____

2. *Content Questions*

◆ Read Genesis 6:1–9:17. What is the symbolic meaning of water in this account? _____

_____

_____

_____

◆ Read Exodus 14:8–31. What is the symbolic meaning of water in this account? _____

_____

_____

_____

◆ Read Romans 6:3–11. How does this passage bring both meanings of water together in Christian baptism? _____

_____

_____

_____

- Read John 3:1–16. How are both symbolic meanings of water brought together by Jesus in his conversation with Nicodemus? _____

_____

_____

_____

_____

_____

- How would you define "catechesis"? _____

_____

_____

_____

_____

_____

- Read Colossians 3:1–17. In the columns below, analyze the symbol of baptism by listing the things the baptized person is to "put off" and those the baptized person is to "put on."

Put off

Put on

- Read Galatians 5:13–25. In the columns below, describe the symbol of baptism by listing all of the acts of the flesh that the baptized Christian is to abandon. Then list the fruits of the Spirit, which represent the new life in the Spirit for the baptized person.

Acts of the flesh   Fruits of the Spirit

_____   _____
_____   _____
_____   _____
_____   _____
_____   _____
_____   _____
_____   _____
_____   _____

3. *Application*

- As you reflect on the New Testament meaning of baptism, how does this symbol challenge your Christian faith and walk?

_____
_____
_____
_____

PART II: GROUP DISCUSSION

The following questions are designed for group discussion. Share the insights you gained from your personal study in Part I.

Write out all answers that group members give to the questions on a chalkboard, a flip chart, or a dry erase board.

1. *Life Connection*
   - Begin your discussion by asking a number of people to share the meaning of the symbol of baptism in their own Christian walk.

2. *Thought Questions*
   - Review Genesis 6:1–9:17 and discuss how this passage points to the destructive nature of water.
   - Review Exodus 14:8–31 and discuss how this passage points to the life-giving power of water.
   - Review John 3:1–16 and discuss how this passage views water as both a destructive power and a life-giving power.
   - Review Romans 6:3–4 and explore how this passage views water as both destructive and life-giving.
   - Make a chart of Colossians 3:1–17 showing what is to be destroyed and what is to be brought to life. Ask each person, "Is there something here you need to bring to destruction? Is there something here you need to bring to life?" Go through each point carefully. Do the same with Galatians 5:13–25.

3. *Application*
   - Evaluate baptism in your church. In prebaptismal training do you adequately teach the destructive and life-giving aspects of the symbolism associated with water?
   - If you have a written baptismal liturgy, read through it looking for the negative and positive symbols associated with water. If your baptismal tradition is oral, recall the spoken words and evaluate them according to the New Testament criteria of destructive and life-giving power.
   - How has this study opened a new understanding of baptism for you? How does that understanding empower you to live in your baptism?

GETTING READY FOR BAPTISM

A Study of Baptism in the Early Church

You have probably heard of Willow Creek Community Church, located in a suburb of Chicago. This church developed a seven-step process of conversion and maturation in the faith. A central component of this seven-step process is the seeker service, which is designed to provide a general introduction into the Christian faith.

Here is a brief outline of the seven steps:

- Every member evangelism. Every member should see himself or herself as a messenger to tell others about Jesus.
- Learning to give witness. Each member must make friends with the unchurched and learn how to share faith with them.
- The seeker service. A Saturday night and Sunday morning service where the unchurched may investigate and hear about the Christian faith in a nonthreatening setting.

The seeker may remain in attendance at the seeker service for an indefinite period of time. Those who make a faith commitment to Jesus Christ are baptized and continue in the steps that follow:

- The new covenant community. This community of believers meets on Wednesday or Thursday night for worship and deeper instruction in the faith.
- Small group ministry. Each new convert is placed in a small group that meets during the week for further instruction and discipleship.
- Discernment of gifts. Each new convert finds his or her gift and puts it to work in the ministry of the church.
- Stewardship. Each person is asked to commit all aspects of life to the service of God as an act of stewardship, not just money.

I have outlined this seven-step process of conversion and maturation in the faith because I want to take you back to the early church, where the word *seeker* was used to describe the converting person. I want to show you the seven steps used by the early church to bring a person into Christ and into the life of the church.

BAPTISM IN THE EARLY CHURCH

Scholars are able to trace the development of a process whereby new people were brought into the church during its first several centuries. While the process began developing in the first century, the flowering of this sevenfold process occurred in the third and fourth centuries.

Remember that this process began during a highly secular period of history. Worship of the emperor was a given, while pagan worship and rites flourished in every city. The church was primarily an underground movement, meeting in catacombs and homes. It was threatened by the emperors who wanted to extinguish it through persecution and severe opposition. But as Tertullian, an early church father, said, "The blood of the martyrs is the seed of the church."

The church grew tremendously in spite of opposition. Scholars of the period argue that one of the major mechanisms in the growth of the church was the seven-step process of baptism and initiation into the church.

Here are the seven steps:
1. Inquiry
2. Rite of welcome
3. Catechumen
4. Rite of election
5. Purification and enlightenment
6. Rite of initiation
7. Mystagogue

The entire seven-step process took two to three years. Three of the seven steps are passage rites that occur in worship, while the other four are lengthier periods of time that allow for growth and development. Next we will examine the seven steps, paying particular attention to the sacred actions that accompany each.

INQUIRY

Those who are interested in the Christian faith are invited to visit with a group of persons from the church. They answer their questions and set before them the call of Christ to "take up your cross and follow me." These persons are known as seekers, and the time of their searching is indefinite.

Rite of Welcome

Those who decide to follow Jesus and prepare for baptism into the death of the old and the birth of the new are presented in the worship of the church. The start of their journey is expressed in three sacred actions. First, they proceed through a ritual of renunciation. In this action they renounce all false gods (meaning the emperor and pagan religions) and affirm their worship of the Triune God alone.

Then they receive the rite of signation. The minister signs their forehead with the sign of the cross in the name of the Father, the Son, and the Holy Spirit. This is known as their "invisible tattoo."

The final sacred action is the invitation to sit among the faithful. This action symbolizes entrance into the church, even though they are not yet allowed to fully participate in the rites of the church such as the eucharist.

Catechumen

The seeker spends two to three years in the study of the faith and in the development of Christian character. The converting person comes to the worship of the church and stays through the sermon. He or she is then dismissed into another place where instruction in the faith is continued. At the end of each period of instruction the catechumen (the seeker who has received instruction; the term *hearer* is also used) receives a laying on of hands. This sacred action, accompanied by a prayer, symbolizes the work of the Holy Spirit in the life of the converting person.

Rite of Election

After the catechumen has successfully completed the instruction and has grown sufficiently in character, a symbolic ritual known as the rite of election takes place in worship.

In this sacred action the hearer is admonished about having been chosen by God. And then the hearer is asked, "Do you choose Jesus?" The hearer answers yes and promptly steps to a book (known as the book of life) and writes his or her name in it. The action is also called the enrollment of names.

Purification and Enlightenment

The rite of election generally occurred on the first Sunday of Lent. The period of purification and enlightenment occurs over the six weeks of Lent. The theme is found in Ephesians 6:12 (KJV), "We wrestle not against flesh and blood, but against principalities, against powers." Every day, the person who is preparing for baptism receives the laying on of hands along with a prayer for purity. In a sense, this stage is the final act of facing the death and destruction of sin that baptism implies, as well as new life in Christ.

THE RITE OF BAPTISM

The primary time for baptism in the early church was on Easter Sunday morning, after the all-night vigil and before the celebration of the eucharist.

Baptism occurred at the rising of the sun (a symbol of resurrection and new life), and it was filled with sacred actions. Those who were to be baptized took off their clothing to symbolize shedding the old life. After baptism they put on new, white robes to symbolize receiving their new life in Christ.

Standing in the water, the one to be baptized was asked, "Do you renounce the devil and all his works?" He or she then turned to the west (the symbol of darkness and the domain of the devil), said "I do," and then spat as if to spit in the face of the devil (a good way to end a relationship). The believing person was then baptized three times—in the name of the Father, in the name of the Son, and in the name of the Holy Spirit. Upon ascending from the water, the newly baptized was anointed with oil as a symbol of receiving the Holy Spirit. Then the converted person entered into the church to receive the eucharist.

MYSTAGOGUE

During the seven weeks of Easter the newly baptized person was instructed in the meaning of the mysteries, primarily the eucharist. The new convert was also encouraged to be involved in the life of the church and to live a life of charity and good actions, pleasing to the Lord.

CONCLUSION

We have seen that the process of coming into Christ and his church in the early period of Christianity was accompanied by powerful sacred actions that delivered the meaning of the transition from an old way of life to a new way of life.

We today are witnessing a shift from a word-driven society to a more visually oriented society. It is appropriate for us to ask how the ancient sevenfold pattern of sacred actions may breathe new life into our churches and into the conversion process of bringing Christian truth and its way of life to the secular society of our day.

The emphasis of putting off the old and putting on the new found in the early church and in a modern church like Willow Creek Community Church points to the need to instruct those who come for baptism in a *process* that allows for the significance of baptism to take hold.

STUDY GUIDE

Read Session 3, "Getting Ready for Baptism,"
before starting the study guide.

PART I: PERSONAL STUDY

Complete the following questions individually.

1. *Life Connection*

♦ Take some time to reflect on your preparation for baptism. What steps did you take? _____

_____

_____

_____

_____

2. *Thought Questions*

♦ Do you think becoming a Christian happens all at once? Or do you think people go through a process? Explain. _____

_____

_____

_____

_____

♦ What is your general impression of the sevenfold process of initiation into the life of the church practiced at Willow Creek Community Church? _____

_____

_____

_____

_____

◆ In the space below all seven steps of the ancient initiation process are listed. Write down your own summary of each.

Inquiry: _____

_____

Rite of welcome: _____

_____

Catechumenate: _____

_____

Rite of election: _____

_____

Purification and enlightenment: _____

_____

Rite of baptism: _____

_____

Mystagogue: _____

_____

◆ In the space below list every *symbol* used in the baptismal process and briefly summarize the meaning of the action.

Symbol   Meaning of the action

_____

_____

_____

_____

_____

3. *Application*

◆ Imagine going through the ancient process of preparing for baptism. How do you think it would influence and shape your spiritual life?

_____

_____

_____

_____

PART II: GROUP DISCUSSION

The following questions are designed for group discussion. Share the insights you gained from your personal study in Part I.

Write out all answers that group members give to the questions on a chalkboard, a flip chart, or a dry erase board.

1. *Life Connection*
- Begin your discussion by asking members of the group to talk about their prebaptismal instruction.

2. *Thought Questions*
- Is becoming a Christian an instantaneous occurrence or a process? Both?
- How do you respond to the sevenfold process of conversion used at Willow Creek Church in the suburb of Chicago?
- Walk through each step in the converting process in the ancient church. Discuss each step thoroughly.
- Discuss each symbol in the ancient process of conversion and baptism. What do they mean? How effective were they?

3. *Application*
- Evaluate the baptismal process used in your church. Is it thorough? Is it effective?
- Use the rest of your time to devise a process for your church to offer all those who come for baptism. What content would you teach? What symbols would you use?
- What impact has this study had on your desire to walk in your baptism?

Do This in Remembrance of Me

A Study in the Sacred Actions of the Lord's Table

The space in the church that my dad pastored was probably very similar to that of most churches in the Protestant tradition. Up front, in view of all the people, was a large pulpit, the symbol of the word of God. Below the pulpit was a beautifully engraved table with the words "Remember Me" carved into the front side.

As far back as I can remember, I read those words, "Remember Me," as a command from Jesus to recall his death. I thought of it as an intellectual exercise, a mindful remembrance to have as I ate the bread and drank from the cup.

It wasn't until I went to seminary that I had my mind and heart opened to the broader meaning of what happens at the table.

We are all aware that coming to the table is a sacred action with many meanings. We are going to explore those meanings in this session.

The Biblical Background

We are all very familiar with the setting in which the Lord's Supper was instituted. It occurred on the night of Passover, the night before Jesus was put to death (Matt 26:17–30). On that night during the meal Jesus took the bread and said, "Take and eat; this is my body." He also took the cup and said, "Drink from it, all of you. This is my blood of the covenant, which is poured out for many for the forgiveness of sins." (vv. 26–28). Let us explore more fully the setting in which the action occurred: a meal.

The Scriptures have a great deal to say about food and the significance of eating. In the beginning we lost our relationship with God over food (Gen 3:1–20) and in the end God will hold the great messianic banquet to celebrate the ultimate victory over the powers of evil (Rev 19:9).

In its broadest sense food is a symbol of God's provision (see Exod 16:1–36 for the example of the manna and the quail) and a sign of relationship (see the many times Jesus eats with others, for example, John 2:1–11; 6:1–14).

Certainly the symbol of provision and relationship lies at the heart of our coming to the table to eat. Jesus made it clear: "I am the bread of life. He who comes to me will never go hungry, and he who believes in me will never be thirsty" (John 6:35). Eating and drinking are acts that carry spiritual significance.

In order to understand more clearly the spiritual meaning of being at the Lord's table, let us turn to the four specific words the New Testament uses to describe the meaning of the sacred actions that happen at the table: the breaking of the bread; the Lord's Supper, Communion, and eucharist.

The Breaking of the Bread

The term *breaking of bread* is first used in Acts 2:42, the earliest description we have of Christian worship.

Used literally, it just means to eat together. Even today some people say, "Come on over to the house and we'll break bread together." Obviously, this is an invitation to enjoy a meal together.

In the early church the term *breaking bread* carried a specific religious meaning that was derived from the experience the apostolic community had with the postresurrection Jesus.

Look at the stories of Jesus and the apostles in the period between his resurrection and ascension. What stands out is that they ate together (Luke 24; John 21:1–14). The key to the spiritual meaning of the breaking of bread is contained in the words of Cleopas and his companion to the disciples in the upper room: "Then the two told what had happened on the way, and *how Jesus was recognized by them when he broke the bread*" (Luke 24:35).

The point is that when Jesus and the apostles were together, they broke bread. Therefore, the breaking of bread became associated with the presence of the resurrected Christ.

The earliest Christian worship described in Acts 2 occurred in a home in the context of a full meal known as the *agape* (love) feast. The believers gathered together to hear the word and break bread in a context of prayer and fellowship. It was a time marked by great joy because the breaking of the bread symbolized the presence of the resurrected Christ among them—the Christ who by his death and resurrection had won a victory over evil and conquered death.

THE LORD'S SUPPER

The next description of table worship occurs in 1 Corinthians 11:17–34. This book is dated at around AD 57, nearly three decades after the resurrection.

Paul describes a problem related to the table of the Lord: Some people were taking resurrection joy too far and getting drunk (1 Cor 11:21). Others were acting like gluttons and eating all the food, leaving others hungry (especially the poor).

So Paul tells them to eat their meal at home and to remember the death. His call to remember the death introduces a note of sobriety into what was otherwise a joyous occasion.

There are four major teachings about the death of Christ that influence our experience at the Lord's table:

- It is a substitutionary death: "this is my blood of the covenant, which is poured out for *many*" (Matt 26:28)
- It is a means of forgiveness: "for the forgiveness of sins" (Matt 26:28)
- It is the ratification of the new covenant: "my blood of the covenant" (Matt 26:28)
- It expresses a future hope (1 Cor 11:26)

The death of Christ, like the Passover, involves both a past event and a future event. The Passover looks back to the Exodus and forward to the promised land. The Lord's Supper looks back to the Christ event and forward to the new heavens and the new earth. "For whenever you eat this bread and drink this cup, you proclaim the Lord's death *until he comes*" (1 Cor 11:26).

At the Lord's table we experience the death of Jesus and anticipate his return.

COMMUNION

The term *Communion* is also a Pauline term. It derives from his statement in 1 Corinthians 10:16–17: "Is not the cup of thanksgiving for which we give thanks a participation in the blood of Christ? And is not the bread that we break a participation in the body of Christ? Because there is one loaf, we, who are many, are one body, for we all partake of the one loaf."

The term *Communion* points to the *koinonia*, the fellowship that we have with one another through eating and drinking the bread and wine.

In the Old Testament, covenant treaties made between warring nations were always sealed with a meal that pointed to the friendship and relationship established on the basis of the covenant (see Gen 26:26–31).

For example, the Passover meal of the Hebrew people remembered their deliverance from Egypt (Exod 12) and served as a meal expressing the covenant and the commitment between God and Israel: "I will take you as my own people, and I will be your God" (Exod 6:7).

This ceremony, the Passover, was to be repeated every year as a sign of the covenant, a oneness Israel had with God.

The meal we eat at the Lord's table, first instituted as the Passover meal, carries the same meaning. Jesus said, "This is my blood of the covenant" (Matt 26:28). Paul reiterates this theme by quoting Jesus (1 Cor 11:25).

The meal that we eat together therefore symbolizes the communion we have with Christ because of the covenant he made with us through the sacrifice of his broken body and shed blood. As we eat together with him and with one another, we signify our relationship to God and our oneness with each other.

Eucharist

The term *eucharist* is generally used by the liturgical church and has come to be associated with Catholics, Orthodox, and Anglicans.

The word is simply the Greek word meaning to give thanks. It is used, for example, by Jesus when he gives thanks for the loaves and the fishes (John 6:11). It is used again by Paul in 1 Corinthians 14:16. The reference here is to the thanksgiving prayer over bread and wine made by the one who is ministering at the table.

The idea is very simple: when we remember the death (Lord's Supper), celebrate the resurrection (break bread), and eat a meal expressing our covenantal relationship with God (Communion), we need to give God thanks (eucharist).

Eucharist is a thank-you. It is our response to God's action of death and resurrection. Therefore, it is a vital and intricate part of what we do when we come together in worship.

Conclusion

This brief study into the New Testament understanding of the Lord's table helps us to see that it is a sacred action full of meaning. In some ways it is related to the meaning of baptism. In baptism we enter the waters to die to sin, and we emerge from the waters to begin a new life in Christ.

In Communion we remember the death that the waters of baptism plunged us into, and we celebrate the resurrection in which we participate by being born anew.

We eat together and commune in fellowship with the risen Lord and with each other. We join the new community of which we are a part to give thanks to God for the work of Jesus Christ.

STUDY GUIDE

Read Session 4, "Do This in Remembrance of Me,"
before starting the study guide.

PART I: PERSONAL STUDY

Complete the following questions individually.

1. *Life Connection*

◆ Remember your earliest experience of Communion. What do you recall from that event? _____

_____

_____

_____

_____

2. *Content Questions*

◆ Read the account of the institution of the Lord's Supper in Matthew 26:17–30. Would you say this account is just a description of what occurred or a prescription for the church? Why?_____

_____

_____

_____

_____

◆ What are the various biblical symbols of food?

_____

_____

_____

_____

_____

◆ Comment on the symbolism associated with food and eating in each of the following passages:

Exodus 16:1–13 _____

_____

John 2:1–11 _____

_____

John 6:35 _____

_____

◆ What are the four terms used in Scripture to refer to the Lord's table?

_____

_____

_____

_____

◆ Read Acts 2:42. Explain the meaning of the breaking of the bread.

_____

_____

_____

_____

_____

◆ Read 1 Corinthians 11:17–34. Explain the meaning of the Lord's Supper.

_____

_____

_____

_____

_____

◆ Read 1 Corinthians 10:16–17. What is the meaning of the word Communion? _____

_____

_____

_____

_____

_____

◆ Read 1 Corinthians 14:16. What is the meaning of the word *eucharist?*

_____

_____

_____

_____

_____

◆ Put these four terms together in your own words to explain the many facets of meaning in the symbols of bread and wine.

_____

_____

_____

_____

_____

_____

3. *Application*

◆ How will this study enrich your next experience of receiving Communion?

_____

_____

_____

_____

_____

PART II: GROUP DISCUSSION

The following questions are designed for group discussion. Share the insights you gained from your personal study in Part I.

Write out all answers that group members give to the questions on a chalkboard, a flip chart, or a dry erase board.

1. *Life Connection*

◆ Begin your discussion by asking various people to recall their earliest experiences of Communion.

2. *Thought Questions*

♦ Is the original account of the institution of the Lord's Supper in Matthew 26:17–30 a description or a prescription? If a prescription, how often should we do the Lord's Supper? Daily, weekly, monthly, yearly? Why?

♦ Discuss the symbolism associated with food in the following Scripture passages:

Exodus 16:7–13

John 2:1–11

John 6:35

♦ Read Acts 2:42 and discuss the meaning of the breaking of bread (have someone do Luke 24:13–35 in a storytelling manner). Ask, "What did you see, hear, feel, or experience from this story that gives you insight into the symbol of the breaking of bread?"

♦ Read 1 Corinthians 11:17–34 and discuss the meaning of the Lord's Supper.

♦ Read 1 Corinthians 10:16 and discuss the meaning of Communion.

♦ Read 1 Corinthians 14:16 and discuss the meaning of eucharist.

♦ Discuss how these four terms give you a new and fuller understanding of bread and wine.

3. *Application*

♦ Evaluate the practice of Communion in your church. Is its meaning fully appreciated, or has it been reduced to one of the four meanings?

♦ What steps can you take to bring a fuller meaning of table worship into your community?

♦ How has this study improved your spiritual life?

THANK-YOU

A Study in the Eucharist of the Early Church

 This past year the speaker during spiritual emphasis week at Wheaton College (where I teach) was a worship thinker and leader, Richard Allen Farmer.

He told an unforgettable story that I want you to hear.

"When I was a kid in our African-American church," he said, "we always sang a song that goes like this."

Waving his right hand in the air he began to sing, "Thank you, thank you, Lord, thank you, thank you, Lord."

"You know," he said, "I thought that song was vacuous and lacking in content until I grew up. When I learned the value of a thank-you, that song took on new meaning."

Have you ever given someone a very special gift? You thought and thought about what to buy. You asked yourself, "What will suit that person best?" And then you proudly presented it. But there never was a thank-you. Do you remember how you felt and what you wondered? Did you fret and say, "Doesn't that person like me? Did I offend? Why haven't I received a thank-you note?"

Thank-yous are important to us, and they are important to God too. In this session we are going to examine the "thank-you" offered by the early church to God, the prayer they called the eucharist, or the great thanksgiving.

BIBLICAL AND HISTORICAL DEVELOPMENT
OF THE PRAYER OF GREAT THANKSGIVING

We saw in the last session that Paul refers to the prayer of blessing in 1 Corinthians 14:16: "If you are praising God with your spirit, how can one who finds himself among those who do not understand say "Amen" to your thanksgiving, since he does not know what you are saying?" Paul is saying, in other words, "say the thank-you in the language of the people so that they can understand and praise God with the mind as well as the spirit."

One of the earliest descriptions of Christian worship outside the New Testament is in a work by Justin Martyr known as the *First Apology* (written about AD 150). In his description of worship he refers to the prayer of thanksgiving in these words:

> Bread is brought and wine and water and the president [minister] . . . sends up prayers and *thanksgivings* to the best of his ability and the congregation assents, saying the Amen.

Justin does not give us the actual content of the prayer of thanksgiving. We have to wait until about AD 215, when a bishop by the name of Hippolytus wrote a work called *The Apostolic Tradition*, a manual for the practice of baptism, the eucharist, and ordination. In this work Hippolytus gives the text of the prayers of thanksgiving used in the early church. According to him this text, or something similar to it, was prayed in the church when he was a boy (this probably takes us back to about AD 150). Below is the full text of that prayer together with some explanatory comments that I have added.

TEXT	COMMENTARY
The Lord be with you. *And all shall say:* And with your spirit.	The *Dominus vobiscum*.
Lift up your hearts. We have lifted them up to the Lord. Let us give thanks to the Lord. It is fitting and right.	In the sursum corda, worship ascends into heaven around the throne of God.
We render thanks to you O God, through your beloved child Jesus Christ, whom in the last times you sent to us as savior and redeemer and angel of your will.	The "preface" to the prayer of thanksgiving is a proclamation.
	At this point we would expect to find the *Sanctus* in which the church joins with the angels and archangels in the heavenly song. This portion of the text is missing.

. . . who is your inseparable Word, through whom you were well pleased. You sent him from heaven into the Virgin's womb; and, conceived in the womb, he was made flesh and was manifested as your Son, being born of the Holy Spirit and the Virgin. Fulfilling your will and gaining for you a holy people, he stretched out his hands when he should suffer, that he might release from suffering those who have believed in you. And when he was betrayed to voluntary suffering that he might destroy death, and break the bonds of the devil, and tread down hell, and shine upon the righteous, and fix the limit, and manifest the resurrection,

. . . he took bread and gave thanks to you saying, "Take, eat, this is my body which shall be broken for you." Likewise also the cup saying, "This is my blood, which is shed for you; when you do this you make my remembrance."

Remembering therefore his death and resurrection, we offer to you the bread and the cup, giving you thanks because you have held us worthy to stand before you and minister to you.

And we ask that you send your Holy Spirit upon the offering of your holy church; that, gathering them into one, you would grant to all who partake of the holy things (to partake) for the fullness of the Holy Spirit for the confirmation of faith in truth.

. . . that we may praise and glorify you through your child Jesus Christ, through whom be glory and honor to you, to the Father and the Son with the Holy Spirit, in your holy Church, both now and to the ages of ages. (Amen.)

The extant text resumes with the eucharistic "prayer of thanksgiving" that recalls God's mighty acts in history, particularly God's act of salvation in Jesus Christ. Note the creedal nature of the prayer as it recounts creation, incarnation, death, resurrection, overthrow of evil, and establishment of the church.

The "words of institution," which repeat the words of Jesus, lie at the heart of the table action.

The *anamnesis* (remembrance) refers not to a mental memory but to a divine action in which Christ, the head of the church, is remembered with the body. The "offering" is the offering of the church's praise, which ministers to God.

In the *epiclesis* ("invocation"), the Holy Spirit is invoked so that those who partake may be confirmed in truth by the work of the Spirit.

The prayer ends with a trinitarian doxology.

LEARNING HOW TO PRAY THE "THANK-YOU" TO GOD

In most churches some kind of thank-you is offered to God at bread and wine. What we want to do in this part of our study is understand how the early church offered its thanks to God in order to improve our own ability to offer thanks.

The prayer of thanksgiving is based on Jewish *berakhah* (blessing) prayers, which were structured around three themes: praise, commemoration, and petition. First, praise is offered to God, then God's works are remembered, and then a petition for future blessing is raised. Note all three parts of the prayer in these words of Jewish prayer: *Blessed be God who brought us out of the land of Egypt; bring us to the promised land.*

Note that the structure of the prayer of thanksgiving in the early church follows the threefold pattern of the ancient Hebrew berakhah prayer. Thus, if you reread the prayer from Hippolytus, you will find praise in the *sursum corda*, commemoration in the eucharistic prayer, words of institution, and *anamnesis*, and petition in the *epiclesis*.

The Christian prayer of thanksgiving is offered to the Triune God: the Father is praised in his character of holiness, the Son is thanked for his work of salvation, and the Holy Spirit is called upon to become present. The prayer ends with a doxology to the Triune God.

CONCLUSION

Let us go back to the opening illustration from the African-American church and reflect on the importance of the thank-you.

Contemporary worship renewal has based its study of the great thanksgiving on the description left for us by Hippolytus. If you are from a mainline church that has access to new resources on worship, look at the prayers of thanksgiving in these resources and allow this lesson to shape your prayer at bread and wine.

If you are from a church that does not have written texts for the prayer of thanksgiving, then meditate on the ancient structure and develop an extemporaneous prayer that praises the Father, remembers the work of the Son, and petitions the Holy Spirit to be present.

STUDY GUIDE

Read Session 5, "Thank-You,"
before starting the study guide.

PART I: PERSONAL STUDY

Complete the following questions individually.

1. *Life Connection*

♦ Remember an occasion when you gave someone a really nice gift but never received a thank-you note or call. How did you feel?

_____

_____

_____

_____

2. *Content Questions*

♦ Read 1 Corinthians 14:16. What is Paul saying in this passage?

_____

_____

_____

_____

♦ Do you think the existence of the prayer of thanksgiving in the early church justifies recovering the prayer of thanksgiving in today's church? Why? _____

_____

_____

_____

♦ Who is Hippolytus and what is *The Apostolic Tradition?* _____

_____

_____

_____

- Read the ancient prayer of thanksgiving on pages 34–36 and then answer the following questions.

- Why is it "fitting and right" to give thanks to God?

  _____

  _____

  _____

  _____

- Why do we give thanks "through Jesus Christ"?

  _____

  _____

  _____

- In the body of the prayer of thanksgiving the early church gave thanks for the history of salvation culminating in Jesus Christ. Can you trace the outline of this "history of salvation"? _____

  _____

  _____

  _____

  _____

- The *anamnesis* says, "you have held us worthy to stand before you and minister to you." How do you interpret that phrase?

  _____

  _____

  _____

  _____

- In the *epiclesis* the prayer calls upon the Holy Spirit. What is the Holy Spirit asked to do? _____

  _____

  _____

- Explain the origin of the thank-you prayer. _____

  _____

  _____

◆ Explain the threefold structure of the thank-you prayer.

_____

_____

_____

_____

3. *Application*

◆ Go back to the text of the ancient eucharistic prayer and pray it slowly and with intention. How does this prayer give you words for saying "thank you" to God? _____

_____

_____

_____

_____

PART II: GROUP DISCUSSION

The following questions are designed for group discussion. Share the insights you gained from your personal study in Part I.

Write out all answers that group members give to the questions on a chalkboard, a flip chart, or a dry erase board.

1. *Life Connection*

◆ Begin your discussion by asking various members to comment on how they feel when a thank-you to a kind act is not forthcoming.

2. *Thought Questions*

◆ Interpret 1 Corinthians 14:16. What is Paul saying in this passage?

◆ Read through the ancient prayer of thanksgiving, then go back and answer the following questions:

  ◆ Why is it "fitting and right" to give thanks to God?

  ◆ Why do we give thanks through Jesus Christ?

- Carefully discuss each line of the history of salvation for which we give thanks. What is the meaning of each phrase?
- What do various members of the class think it means to say "you have held us worthy to stand before you and minister to you"? How is a thank-you a ministry to God?
- What is the Holy Spirit asked to do? How can the ministry of the Holy Spirit be accomplished?
- How is the ancient thank-you prayer structured around the Trinity?

3. *Application*
- Evaluate the Communion prayers in your worship. If they are written, study them for parallels to the ancient prayer. If they are of an oral tradition, try to remember the content and structure for evaluation.
- Prepare a Communion service for your church that reflects the ancient trinitarian structure and truly gives thanks.
- How has this study affected your spiritual life?

PART II

SACRED

ACTIONS

COMMONLY

ACCEPTED BY

THE CHURCH

I BELIEVE

A Study in Confirmation

I grew up in a church that did not practice confirmation, so it was an unfamiliar ritual to me. As I grew older and gained more experience in a variety of churches, I soon learned that not all churches, including the church of my upbringing, had rituals that could be interpreted as a kind of confirmation.

Confirmation is generally associated with churches that practice infant baptism. At confirmation, a person is willing to announce before God and the church, "I personally believe that Jesus Christ is Savior and Lord of my life, and I promise that I will follow him in faith and works of love." At that point the confirmand's relationship with God becomes more alive through the presence of the Holy Spirit.

In my church upbringing baptism and confirmation were combined. The word *confirmation* was not used, and baptism was the ritual through which a person made a public profession of faith. Because the Holy Spirit was received during this experience, confirmation came from above and within. But Christians are prone to wander from the straight and narrow, and so my church had rededication calls on Sunday nights and especially on youth retreats. These rededication services included rituals through which the wanderer gave his or her life back to Jesus and found new empowerment by the Holy Spirit. While we did not have a ritual called *confirmation*, we did have a ritual that confirmation is intended to accomplish—a personal commitment to Jesus Christ.

BIBLICAL BASIS AND HISTORICAL DEVELOPMENT OF CONFIRMATION

The Bible itself does not use the word *confirmation*, but the theological roots for the idea are found in Ephesians 1:13: "And you also were included in Christ when you heard the word of truth, the gospel of your salvation. Having believed, you were marked in him with a seal, the promised Holy Spirit."

Notice that there are two parts to the action, the human part, "having believed," and the divine part, "you were marked in him with a seal, the promised Holy Spirit."

The early church associated the reception of the Holy Spirit with baptism. The event of baptism included two rituals: water baptism and the anointing of oil for the reception of the Holy Spirit. After the hearer had been baptized, he or she came up out of the water and received an anointing with oil that served as the outward sacred action of the Spirit. The earliest description of the Ephesians 1:13 ritual is recorded by Hippolytus in *The Apostolic Tradition* (written about AD 215). For the anointing of oil, the minister anointed a person's forehead, eyes, nose, ears, mouth, and collar bones with the sign of the cross and oil to indicate the anointing of the whole person with the Holy Spirit.

This ritual was so powerful and meant so much that the newly baptized person would sometimes take a bottle of oil and pour it over the entire body. Rituals in the early church were lavish and rich. They were not stingy and restrained, as rituals in many churches seem today.

Later Developments

In the early church it was a standard practice to baptize adults by immersion (there are some examples of infant baptism, and baptism by sprinkling or pouring).

However, the practice of the early church changed because of two events. The first was the conversion of Constantine in AD 311 and the second was the rise of infant baptism. They are connected.

First, the conversion of Constantine resulted in an immense change for the church. For three centuries the church was a persecuted minority, hunted by the state and forced for the most part to meet clandestinely. Entrance into the church was demanding and rigorous. After the conversion of Constantine, however, the whole Roman Empire became Christian (in name at least). By 380 the emperor Theodosius declared Christianity to be the only legitimate religion in the empire.

One consequence of this drastic change was the wholesale introduction of infant baptism. Because nearly everyone was Christian in name at least, all children were to be baptized into the church. In time, the ritual of the anointing with oil as a seal of the Holy Spirit was separated from the ritual of baptism. The original anointing with oil for the Holy Spirit became "confirmation," the act of personally affirming the meaning of baptism. For that reason, the ancient practice fell into disuse, and confirmation became a ritual of its own.

CONTEMPORARY DEVELOPMENTS

In worship renewal today there is a strong trend to return to the practice of the early church, in the free church tradition and among the liturgical churches as well. Let me give you an example from a Catholic church.

I recently saw a video of a service of baptism and anointing of oil for the sealing of the Spirit filmed in a Catholic church in Paradise, Texas. I was amazed at how extravagant their rituals were. When the newly baptized woman came up out of the water, the oil of confirmation was not just gingerly put on her head. Instead, the minister held a canister of oil and poured it until the woman's head was literally soaked in oil. Then the minister smeared the oil all over her face, all around her eyes, nose, ears, and mouth. Days after the service the woman exclaimed, "It was wonderful. It was like the Holy Spirit was just taking over my whole life. I could feel the presence of the Spirit. For days the smell of the oil and the feeling of the special sense of the Holy Spirit's presence lingered about me. I think about that experience all of the time." For her and the people of this church, confirmation was a powerful experience of the work of the Holy Spirit.

CONCLUSION

Confirmation is one of those sacred actions that has undergone considerable change throughout the history of the church. The symbol does mean to personally confirm the faith. But many churches have found it to be an ineffective symbol for those baptized as infants and been confirmed at age twelve.

For this reason, some churches are going back to the early Christian tradition of adult baptism, which includes symbols of personal, confirming faith as part of its ritual.

Since this symbol is under considerable discussion, its current use in the church is not characterized by a unity of understanding.

The one conviction that brings almost everyone together is the affirmation that faith requires personal confirmation verbally and symbolically.

STUDY GUIDE

Read Session 6, "I Believe,"
before starting the study guide.

PART I: PERSONAL STUDY

Complete the following questions individually.

1. *Life Connection*

◆ If your church practiced confirmation and if you went through confirmation studies and became confirmed, tell about your experience. If your church did not practice confirmation, but held other rituals, such as dedication calls, describe them. _____

_____

_____

_____

_____

_____

2. *Content Questions*

◆ Read Ephesians 1:13. Explain why this verse is usually associated with confirmation or an act that accomplishes the same end. _____

_____

_____

_____

_____

_____

◆ How was the symbol of confirmation accomplished in the early church?

_____

_____

_____

_____

_____

_____

◆ What two events in the early Christian era brought about a change in the form of confirmation?

a. _____

b. _____

◆ How did the conversion of Constantine change the church?

_____

_____

_____

_____

_____

◆ How did the rise of infant baptism after the conversion of Constantine cause confirmation to become separated from baptism?

_____

_____

_____

_____

◆ Describe how the Roman Catholic church of Paradise, Texas, has recovered the original symbolic power of anointing with oil for the filling of the Holy Spirit and the confirmation of faith.

_____

_____

_____

_____

_____

3. *Application*

◆ Describe both the words and the actions (symbols) you went through to confirm your own faith in Jesus Christ as Lord. _____

_____

_____

_____

_____

PART II: GROUP DISCUSSION

The following questions are designed for group discussion. Share the insights you gained from your personal study in Part I.

Write out all answers that group members give to the questions on a chalkboard, a flip chart, or a dry erase board.

1. *Life Connection*

♦ Begin your discussion by polling the class. How many went through a formal confirmation class? How many went through a more informal set of confirming rituals and symbols? Encourage a number of people to speak of their various confirming rituals.

2. *Thought Questions*

♦ Discuss Ephesians 1:13 and the importance of the human side of faith and the symbol of divine action. Explore how the various forms of confirmation either fulfilled or did not fulfill these two sides of a true confirming of faith.

♦ Discuss the symbols of the early church. Should our symbolism today be more lavish?

♦ Discuss how the early form of confirmation, which was associated with baptism, underwent a significant change after the period of the early church.

♦ Discuss the current recovery of the early church approach to confirmation with oil. Is this a positive move? Or should the church abandon confirmation altogether?

3. *Application*

♦ Evaluate confirmation (or alternative) practice in your church today. How is it done? Is it effective?

♦ How should we change the practice of confirmation (or its alternative) in our churches today?

- What would you teach as the *content* for confirmation? How is this content symbolized in your worship?
- How has this lesson made an impact on your spiritual life?

FORGIVE ME

A Study in Reconciliation

 In recent years a whole new profession called mediation has developed. The enormous number of disputes in modern life has necessitated the emergence of such a profession.

There are a number of people close to me who function as mediators. For example, my wife, who is an attorney, took mediation training to use in her profession. I have another friend doing mediation for divorcing couples. Another friend does mediation in corporate business and education. And a minister friend recently retired from his church to do full-time mediation with churches in dispute with their ministers or divided over the direction the church is taking.

Disputes, of course, are nothing new. We can trace disputes all the way back to Cain and Abel (Gen 4:1–8). Certainly biblical history is characterized by as many disputes as the divided church.

In this session we will consider how the church has handled disputes. This leads us to the sacred action known as reconciliation.

BIBLICAL BACKGROUND

The Bible is full of examples of situations that cry out for reconciliation, above all the breakdown of relationship between God and God's creatures. But God set about to bring reconciliation with creation.

This great biblical drama also includes other dramas of reconciliation, for example, the creation story, the story of Noah and the flood, and the story of Israel. All are stories of broken relationships in need of repair.

The apostle Paul developed a language of reconciliation. Consider, for example, these passages:

2 Corinthians 5:18: "All this is from God, who reconciled us to himself through Christ and gave as the ministry of reconciliation."

Colossians 1:19–20: "God was pleased . . . to reconcile to himself all things."

Ephesians 2:16: "In this one body to reconcile both of them to God through the cross."

THE EARLY CHURCH

The early church saw the experience of reconciliation in baptism, in the seal of the Spirit (in baptism and later in confirmation), and in the eucharist. These were the primary sacred actions through which God communicated and persons received reconciliation with God.

With time, the church encountered problems in dealing with people who committed grievous sins but then wanted to return to the church (grievous sins included rejection of the faith in the face of persecution, as well as adultery and murder).

The church developed a system of penitence that was integrated into the cycle of preparation for baptism. They entered the process on Ash Wednesday through a confession, followed by a lengthy time of penance and spiritual renewal (this could last a lifetime, depending on the nature of the sin). The penitent, when deemed ready, was reintroduced into the life of the church during the Holy Week. Along with those preparing for baptism, the penitent would go through confessions and absolutions and finally be received into the church and allowed to participate in the eucharist.

This ritual gave rise to the penitential system of the Roman Catholic Church, which involves (1) contrition for the sin, (2) satisfaction for the sin (anything from prayer to fasting and abstinences), and (3) absolution declared by the priest.

At its best, the system of penitence resulted in a sense that atonement had been made and guilt had been removed. But at its worst, the system of penance in the late medieval era generated a sense of reconciliation based on works and a hypocrisy of confession followed by irrelevant acts of satisfaction to achieve a priest's absolution. The system generated a false experience of Christianity, to which the Reformers responded by rejecting penance. The Reformers introduced an approach to forgiveness based on genuine repentance before God, followed by a changed life. This action took place in private personal prayer and did not depend on confession to a priest.

RECONCILIATION TODAY

Today Catholics recognize that the system of penance developed in the medieval church is inadequate because it tends to make reconciliation a matter of following the rules and not a matter of the heart.

On the other hand, Protestants are recognizing the need to be more specific than simply saying, "Go confess your sin to God."

Consequently, a mutual approach to reconciliation has been developed among both Catholics and Protestants. It consists of three sacred actions:

◆ A dialogue is set up between the person who has committed the sin and the minister. This dialogue may continue for any number of sessions. In this setting the penitent makes a full confession of sin (liturgical rites for penitence are available in the recently published worship resources of most churches), and the minister counsels the person, using Scripture as a guide.

◆ A second form of reconciliation occurs when a group of persons come together. In this communal setting the people reflect on pertinent Scripture, followed by a form of confession and words of forgiveness proclaimed by the minister. The confessions are individual and specific, and the words of forgiveness are directed to each person individually as opposed to the whole group.

◆ A third form, or sacred action, is similar in format. The main difference is that the confessional words are communal, not individual. The words of forgiveness are directed toward the group generally, not specifically to each individual.

All of the reconciliation situations described above may be expressed through a number of sacred actions. For example, the penitent may kneel during the confession, and the minister, at the words of forgiveness, may lay hands on the head of the penitent. Other rituals, such as the sign of the cross and the embrace of the kiss of peace, may also be used to convey the achievement of reconciliation.

CONCLUSION

Reconciliation with God or between opposing parties is much more than an intellectual agreement. It is more than something that happens in the head. It is an experience of the whole person.

For that reason, reconciliation needs both word and symbol. Protestant churches have been churches of the word for four centuries. But they are now learning that symbols speak, and they play an important part in reconciling us to God and to each other.

STUDY GUIDE

Read Session 7, "Forgive Me,"
before starting the study guide.

PART I: PERSONAL STUDY

Complete the following questions individually.

1. *Life Connections*

♦ Recall a dispute you have had with another person, an insurance company, or a business. How was this dispute settled?

_____

_____

_____

_____

2. *Content Questions*

♦ Use your own words to explain how the message of reconciliation lies at the heart of the Bible. _____

_____

_____

_____

_____

♦ Explain how each story relates to reconciliation.
The Noah story _____

_____

_____

_____

The story of Israel _____

_____

_____

_____

♦ How do the following Scriptures speak to reconciliation? (Look up the larger context.)

2 Corinthians 5:18 _____

_____

Colossians 1:19–20 _____

_____

Ephesians 2:16 _____

_____

♦ In what way do the following sacred actions relate to reconciliation?

Baptism _____

Seal of the Spirit (confirmation) _____

Eucharist _____

♦ How did the early church deal with people who had committed grievous sin and then wanted to repent and return to the church?

_____

_____

_____

_____

_____

♦ What are the three parts of the Catholic penitential system?

a. _____

b. _____

c. _____

◆ Describe the result of the penitential system at its *best* and at its *worst*.

Best _____

_____

_____

Worst _____

_____

_____

◆ Describe the Protestant Reformers' approach to penitence and reconciliation. _____

_____

_____

_____

_____

◆ Describe three approaches to reconciliation used in churches today.

a. _____

_____

b. _____

_____

c. _____

_____

3. *Application*

◆ Is there a relationship or situation in your life that needs reconciliation today? Which of the sacred actions discussed in this lesson would be most suitable for this matter? _____

_____

_____

_____

_____

PART II: GROUP DISCUSSION

The following questions are designed for group discussion. Share the insights you gained from your personal study in Part I.

Write out all answers that group members give to the questions on a chalkboard, a flip chart, or a dry erase board.

1. *Life Connection*

♦ Begin your discussion by asking various members of the class to comment on how they resolve disputes in their lives.

2. *Thought Questions*

♦ Discuss how the overall message of the Bible is one of reconciliation.

♦ Discuss how reconciliation occurs in the stories of the flood and of Israel.

♦ Review the message of reconciliation in the following passages of Scripture by reading and discussing them in their larger context:

2 Corinthians 5:18	(Read and comment on 2 Cor 5:11–21.)
Colossians 1:19–20	(Read and comment on Col 1:15–23.)
Ephesians 2:16	(Read and comment on Eph 2:1–22.)

♦ Discuss how baptism, confirmation, and eucharist all work as sacred actions that result in reconciliation.

♦ Compare the Roman Catholic penitential approach to reconciliation with the Protestant conviction that all sinners can go directly to God without a mediator. What are the strengths and weaknesses of each?

♦ Discuss each of the three contemporary approaches to reconciliation. In what kind of situation does each one work best?

3. *Application*

♦ Is there a situation in your church that needs reconciliation? Discuss how it should be handled, based on the study in this session.

♦ Ask, "How can each person in this class use one of the approaches to reconciliation suggested in this study in his or her life?"

I Do

A Study in Marriage

I spent the first seven years of my life in Africa, where my parents were missionaries. One of my most vivid memories is of a wedding my father conducted. Everyone from the village was present in the thatched-roof church awaiting the moment. Soon the procession of bride and groom was completed, as well as the opening words. Then my father addressed the woman with the words, "Do you take this man to be your lawful wedded husband?" His question was followed by a long silent pause. Everyone waited breathlessly to hear the words "I do." They were shocked to hear the word "no" as the woman turned and walked down the aisle and out of the church.

Christians consider marriage to be a sacred action, a coming together of a man and a woman in the context of a Christian assembly to vow to live together before God. But what does marriage mean and why are its actions sacred?

THE HEBREW BASIS OF MARRIAGE

In Hebrew thought marriage is rooted in the doctrine of creation. God is Creator, and man and woman are made in God's image (Gen 1:27; 5:1–2). Because they are created *together* and find their equality with each other as human beings, man and woman are to marry and become as if one person (Gen 2:23–24).

This image of marriage is carried out in the relationship that God established in the covenant with Israel. The ceremony marking the covenantal agreement between God and Israel, much like a marriage ceremony, includes an oath of fidelity and a symbol of union (Exod 24:1–8).

Throughout the history of Israel the relationship between Israel and Yahweh is repeatedly referred to in terms of a marriage. Four of Israel's great prophets—Hosea, Jeremiah, Isaiah, and Ezekiel—speak of the relationship in marital terms. The prophet Hosea is married to an unfaithful wife and from that hurtful situation he speaks of the pain God experiences from the unfaithfulness of Israel. Thus in this instance marriage serves as a prophetic symbol.

THE NEW TESTAMENT BASIS OF MARRIAGE

This Hebrew concept of prophetic symbolism (that marriage bespeaks the spiritual relationship between God and God's people) is continued in the New Testament, but with a minor change.

Marriage is no longer the symbol of relationship between Yahweh and Israel, but it becomes a prophetic symbol of the relationship between Christ and the church (see Eph 5:21–33).

The central image is that Jesus Christ gave himself to the church (Eph 5:25). His self-giving love serves as the primary sacred action of marriage. As a consequence of Christ's self-giving, the marriage relationship is most thoroughly Christian (i.e., a prophetic symbol) when (1) the wife submits to her husband as the church submits to Jesus Christ (6:22–24) and (2) the husband serves the wife in *the same way* that Christ loved the church and gave himself up for it (Eph 6:25).

The result of this kind of marriage is the mystery of mutual service. It is not that the man lords it over the woman and tells her what to do, or vice versa, but that in mutual submission husband and wife work out a relationship that is a symbol of Christ and the church. Paul appropriately ends this discussion with the words "this is a profound mystery" (6:32).

MARRIAGE: COVENANT OR SACRAMENT

The New Testament image of marriage as an image of the relationship between Christ and the church has shaped the affirmation of marriage as a sacrament. To affirm that marriage is a sacrament is to say with the ancient church that marriage is the context in which God's grace is experienced. This means that marriage, because it is the primary human experience of the spiritual relationship between Christ and the church, is a sacred trust that cannot be broken. Consequently, in the Catholic and Orthodox churches marriage is viewed as a sacrament and divorce is difficult to obtain.

The Old Testament notion that marriage is based on a covenant—an agreement between two parties—suggests that the covenant is more easily broken. Even as Israel broke covenant with God, so in our marriages we break covenant with each other. Divorce on the basis of a broken covenant is easier to obtain in the Protestant church, which generally rejects the notion of marriage as a sacrament. However, the ideal view of covenant in Protestant circles is that a covenant should not be broken. Still, the Protestant view is more lenient toward divorce than the sacramental view, which argues for an unbreakable relationship based on Christ and the church.

CONCLUSION

Today we live in a society where the cycle of divorce and remarriage and divorce again is becoming altogether too common. This is equally true in the church.

Perhaps we need to reexamine the biblical basis of marriage and model for our children and our children's children a view of marriage that draws on both the Hebrew and the Christian images of a man and a woman leaving father and mother to become one.

STUDY GUIDE

Read Session 8, "I Do,"
before starting the study guide.

PART I: PERSONAL STUDY

Complete the following questions individually.

1. *Life Connection*
- How serious is the wedding vow? Is it really "until death do us part," or are there reasons the vow can be set aside? _____

_____

_____

_____

2. *Content Questions*
- Explain the Hebrew concept of marriage, as it is rooted in the doctrine of creation. _____

_____

_____

_____

- Explain how the image of marriage as a covenant between two parties is expressed in the covenant between God and Israel (Exod 24:1–8).

_____

_____

_____

- Quickly skim through the book of Hosea and comment on how Hosea's marriage to a faithless woman is a prophetic symbol of Israel's relationship with God. _____

_____

_____

_____

- Explain how the New Testament symbol of marriage shifts from Israel and Yahweh to Christ and the church. _____

  _____

  _____

  _____

  _____

- Read Ephesians 5:21–33. Has this passage been misinterpreted by those who argue the husband should lord it over the wife?

  _____

  _____

  _____

  _____

- What is the primary sacred action of marriage?

  _____

  _____

  _____

  _____

- What are two ingredients of a thoroughly Christian marriage?

  a. _____

  _____

  b. _____

  _____

- Explain the argument for marriage as a *covenant*.

  _____

  _____

  _____

  _____

- Explain the argument for marriage as a *sacrament*.

  _____

  _____

  _____

  _____

3. *Application*

◆ Do you think marriage should be seen as a covenant or a sacrament? Explain your answer. _____

_____

_____

_____

_____

_____

PART II: GROUP DISCUSSION

The following questions are designed for group discussion. Share the insights you gained from your personal study in Part I.

Write out all answers that group members give to the questions on a chalkboard, a flip chart, or a dry erase board.

1. *Life Connection*

◆ Begin your discussion by asking various members of the group to respond to the phrase "until death do us part." Are there situations in which the marriage vow can be set aside? Or is marriage forever, no matter what the circumstances? Ask for examples.

2. *Thought Questions*

◆ Explain the Hebrew concept of marriage.

◆ Read Exodus 24:1–8. How does the covenant between God and Israel resemble the marriage ceremony? What are the two common elements?

◆ Discuss Hosea as an Old Testament example of "prophetic symbol."

◆ How does the New Testament understanding of marriage differ from the Hebrew understanding?

◆ Read Ephesians 5:21–33. Discuss how this passage presents a Christian view of marriage.

3. *Application*

- Obtain a copy of the marriage ceremony used in your church. Read through it, commenting on the words and phrases. Does the ceremony view marriage as a covenant or a sacrament?

- Discuss how truly understanding and living out Ephesians 5:21–33 would change your marriage.

SET APART

A Study in Ministry

In my travels among churches I have observed that some churches are controlled from the top. Other churches have no specific person in control, and they experience a freedom of the entire community in action. I don't mean to suggest that these churches have no leaders. They do. But they lead by consensus, not fiat.

The difference between a controlling clergy and a church body experiencing a oneness in action is usually related to the view of the ministry held by that particular church.

If ministry is restricted to clergy and if the clergy is controlling (for whatever reason), then the church's action as a body is stifled. The most controlling clergy seem to be those who approach the church as a corporate business. Like corporate executives, they want to call the shots and have everyone jump to their commands.

This approach to church ministry fails to recognize that the church is a body and that everyone in the church, from the oldest to the youngest, is a minister. Churches are not to function as corporate businesses because the church is the body of Christ, not a business. Christ alone is the head of the church, and he directs the ministries given to the church by the Spirit.

THE NEW TESTAMENT BACKGROUND

The most important passage of Scripture dealing with the body of Christ is 1 Corinthians 12. The items in the following list capture its essential teaching. Take some time to reflect on their implications.

- "There are different kinds of gifts, but the same Spirit." (v. 4)
- "To each one the manifestation of the Spirit is given for the common good." (v. 7)
- "The body is a unit, though it is made up of many parts." (v. 12)
- "You are the body of Christ, and each of you is a part of it." (v. 27)

In this same passage Paul lists some of the ministries within the body (v. 28). It is important to note that this list is partial, not exhaustive.

- Apostles
- Prophets
- Teachers
- Workers of miracles
- Those having the gift of healing
- Those able to help others
- Those with gifts of administration
- Those speaking in different kinds of tongues

Paul makes it clear that no one person is expected to do everything. Each person instead works as a part of the body, as he taught in verses 14–26. He strengthens his argument by asking: "Are all apostles? Are all prophets? Are all teachers? Do all work miracles? Do all have gifts of healing? Do all speak in tongues? Do all interpret?" (vv. 29–30)

Paul uses the rhetorical method in these questions. He does not answer them because the answer is obvious.

But then he moves on to state that there is one gift that everyone has—the gift of love (12:31; 13:1–13).

TONGUES AND PROPHECY

In chapter 14 Paul tackles a controversial issue—speaking in tongues. It is clear that Paul himself spoke in tongues and that tongues was one of the gifts of ministry. Yet he does not say everyone should speak in tongues. He says everyone should exercise the gift of love. Paul's view of tongues may be best captured in these words: "I thank God I speak in tongues more than all of you. But in the church I would rather speak five intelligible words to instruct others than ten thousand words in a tongue" (14:18).

Paul also addresses the matter of prophecy. "Follow the way of love," he says, "and eagerly desire spiritual gifts, especially the gift of prophecy" (14:1). Prophecy, he says, is for unbelievers and may be exercised in the church in worship, while tongues is for private edification and is directed toward God. He concludes his argument with these words:

So if the whole church comes together and everyone speaks in tongues, and some who do not understand or some unbelievers come in, will they not say that you are out of your mind? But if an unbeliever or someone who does not understand comes in while everybody is prophesying, he will be convinced by all that he is a sinner and will be judged by all, and the secrets of his heart will be laid bare. So he will fall down and worship God, exclaiming, "God is really among you!" (1 Cor 14:23–25)

ORDERLY WORSHIP

The use of spiritual gifts by all the people in ministry raises the question of order in worship. Paul certainly implies that we need to bring all our gifts to worship when he says "when you come together, everyone has a hymn, or a word of instruction, a revelation, a tongue or an interpretation. All of these must be done for the strengthening of the church" (1 Cor 14:26).

Paul then gives some instruction on the order of worship and ends with an order: "Everything should be done in a fitting and orderly way" (v. 40).

WHAT ABOUT THE ORDAINED MINISTRY?

Most churches today are characterized by an ordained clergy. Where do they come from? What is their place in a church that is called to function as a body?

The word *ordination* does not appear in the Scripture, but the idea of setting certain persons aside for a particular ministry is present. The terms *elder, bishop,* and *deacon* are used, and each has a different function.

The office of elder was borrowed with some modification from the Jewish synagogue. In the synagogue the elder was the custodian of the Mosaic law and the primary teacher of the people. Today the minister of the church is sometimes referred to as its teaching elder (see Acts 11:30; 14:23).

The word *bishop* means "overseer" (see its usage in Acts 20:28). Some argue that the office of bishop is separate from the office of elder (Episcopal Church), while others argue the office of bishop and elder are interchangeable (Presbyterian Church). The New Testament is not absolutely clear on the matter (see 1 Tim 3:1–13).

The office of deacon is a creation of the New Testament church and is not borrowed from any Jewish prototype. The deacon's role is that of service (see Acts 6:1–6).

In this brief survey we cannot solve the problem of ministry that exists among the churches. Some churches argue that because we are all ministers, there should be no ordained ministry (Plymouth Brethren), other churches are ruled by a bishop (Catholic, Orthodox, Anglican, Lutheran, Mennonite). Others are ruled by a presbytery (Presbyterian, Reformed), and some local churches are ruled by deacons (Baptist).

CONCLUSION

The real focus of this session has been on the gifts that all of us bring to ministry.

While the overall subject of ministry pertaining to clergy is not absolutely clear either in Scripture or in church history (evident by the divisions in the church over this matter), what is clear is the need for all of us to discover our own gifts of ministry and to bring them to life in the work of the church, allowing our gifts to be empowered by the Spirit in the sacred actions of worship.

STUDY GUIDE

Read Session 9, "Set Apart,"
before starting the study guide.

PART I: PERSONAL STUDY

Complete the following questions individually.

1. *Life Connection*

 ◆ Have you been in a church that was controlled by clergy? Describe that
 situation. _____

 _____

 _____

 _____

 _____

 ◆ Have you been in a church that was governed by consensus, where everyone was viewed as a minister? Describe that situation. _____

 _____

 _____

 _____

 _____

 _____

2. *Content Questions*

 ◆ Read 1 Corinthians 12:1–30. Find as many statements as you can in this
 passage that teach that the church is a body. Write them out.

 _____

 _____

 _____

 _____

 _____

 _____

 _____

◆ Explain the following ministries in the New Testament church. What does each do? Is there a modern counterpart?

Apostles _____

Prophets _____

Teachers _____

Elders _____

Bishops _____

Deacons _____

Workers of miracles _____

Those having the gift of healing _____

Those able to help others _____

Those with gifts of administration _____

Those speaking in different kinds of tongues _____

◆ Read 1 Corinthians 13:1–13. While not everyone has every gift, everyone is to have the gift of love. According to this text, what are some of the ways the gift of love is exhibited? _____

_____

_____

_____

_____

_____

_____

◆ Use your own words to describe Paul's understanding of tongues in worship.

_____

_____

_____

_____

_____

_____

◆ Use your own words to describe Paul's understanding of the place of prophecy in worship. _____

_____

_____

_____

_____

◆ In Paul's mind everyone makes a contribution to worship. What is the goal of this body ministry as expressed in 1 Corinthians 14:26?

_____

_____

_____

3. *Application*

◆ What is the gift you bring to worship and how do you use it?_____

_____

_____

_____

PART II: GROUP DISCUSSION

The following questions are designed for group discussion. Share the insights you gained from your personal study in Part I.

Write out all answers that group members give to the questions on a chalkboard, a flip chart, or a dry erase board.

1. *Life Connection*

◆ Begin your discussion by asking members of the class to give experiences of clergy-driven churches and churches ordered by consensus.

2. *Thought Questions*

◆ Read through 1 Corinthians 12:1–31. Find the many phrases in this chapter that speak of body life and the ministry of all God's people in worship. How does your church measure up?

◆ Read through 1 Corinthians 13:1–13. Find the phrases that speak of the common gift of love. How does your church measure up?

◆ Read through 1 Corinthians 14:1–40. How does your church deal with the issue of tongues? Prophecy? Should the comment about the silence of women be a universal norm? Or do you think the comment was made to address a particular issue at a particular time?

3. *Application*

◆ Take some time to talk about each person's gift. Write those gifts on the board. Then ask, "How can each person's gift be used more effectively in worship?"

◆ Discuss whether this church is clergy centered in ministry or body driven. What steps need to be taken to experience body worship?

◆ How can everyone fulfill the gift of love?

HEAL ME

A Study in Anointing

Back in the early 1970s a friend of mine was devastated to discover that he had cancer. In desperation he called upon the elders of the church he pastored to anoint him with oil and pray for his healing. In the early 1970s there were not many churches that had recovered the New Testament practice of anointing with oil, so the board of elders was apprehensive. The anointing with oil was something new for them, and they were not quite sure what to make of it. So they reluctantly turned down the pastor's request. Fortunately, another church sent a team of people to pray for the minister. Today he is enjoying good health and pastors a church elsewhere.

In the years since my friend's request, anointing of oil with the laying on of hands have become increasingly common. Let us look at this phenomenon and ask how it may be used in the church today.

THE BIBLICAL BASIS FOR ANOINTING WITH OIL

Oil has always had a number of purposes. In ancient times it was burned in lamps for light, was used in bread and other foods, and was applied to the body as a healing agent as well.

In Israel it was used as a sign to set people apart for service to the Lord. Kings and prophets were anointed with oil when they were commissioned for their callings. For this reason they were often referred to as "the Lord's anointed" (see 1 Sam 16:6; 24:6, 10; 2 Sam 23:1; Ps 2:2).

Like the kings and prophets of the Old Testament, Christ is called God's anointed one (Acts 4:26, 27). As the anointed one, Jesus anoints others with his healing power.

The healing power of Jesus is associated with his work as Lord and Savior of the world. He came to overthrow the powers of evil, including the sickness that permeates the world—not only the sickness of the body but also the sickness of the soul and the emotions. Jesus heals the sickness of society represented in the hate, greed, and violence of the world. Jesus, by his death and resurrection, is the great healer and deliverer of the world.

Consequently, the New Testament church recognized the healing power of anointing with oil in his name. James describes the practice of the church: "Is any one of you sick? He should call the elders of the church to pray over him and anoint him with oil in the name of the Lord" (Jas 5:14).

OTHER REFERENCES TO ANOINTING

Anointing is not limited to illness. For example, Paul tells the Corinthian church that God has anointed him and sealed him, giving him the Holy Spirit in his heart as a pledge (2 Cor 1:21–22). John writes to the first-century church, "You have an anointing from the Holy One" (1 John 2:20).

Thus the church has expanded its understanding and use of oil beyond illness to other concerns, such as anointing for personal blessing and/or empowerment in ministry.

ANOINTING WITH OIL TODAY

In worship renewal today the anointing of oil is primarily used for wellness or empowerment. Anointing takes place in the church in worship and in private in the hospital or home.

In worship the anointing of oil best occurs during the eucharist or in the alternative service of thanksgiving. People walk forward to receive the bread and wine; the entire congregation is singing songs of the death, resurrection, and exaltation of Jesus. These songs proclaim Jesus as victor over sin, death, and all the powers of evil. The person who has received the bread and wine stops at an appointed station where someone with the gift of healing anoints and prays for him or her.

As the congregant stands or kneels, the anointing one puts oil on his or her forehead in the name of the Father, the Son, and the Holy Spirit (making the sign of the cross). Closing his or her hands around the person's ears, the anointing one then prays a prayer something like this: May the Holy Spirit bring healing into your life—mind, body, and soul. And may you be filled with the presence of Jesus.

The one doing the anointing may then offer the anointed one the peace of Christ. And the anointed one may return to his or her seat to sing and pray with the others.

When someone is sick at home or in the hospital, the ministers of the anointing go to that person with oil, read a psalm or another appropriate passage of Scripture, and perform the anointing.

I have been involved in both kinds of anointing. In workshops where I conduct a worship service, there is always an anointing of oil together with the eucharist. Usually 80 percent of those attending, most of whom have never received an anointing with oil, will come to be anointed. I have received many letters and communications from people who have received a healing in their lives or empowerment in their ministries.

Whenever I go to the hospital to visit a sick friend, I anoint that person with oil and pray a prayer similar to the one above. Persons whom I have anointed report a peace and a strengthening from the sacred action of oil, the laying on of hands, and the prayer of healing.

CONCLUSION

We live in a broken world. That is the bad news that the gospel brings. But the good news of the gospel is that because of the death and resurrection of Jesus, healing and restoration has been brought to the brokenness of our lives.

For that reason the sacred action of anointing with oil—in worship, in the home, and in the hospital—demonstrates in a tangible way God's sacred action of healing and empowerment in our lives.

STUDY GUIDE

Read Session 10, "Heal Me,"
before starting the study guide.

PART I: PERSONAL STUDY

Complete the following questions individually.

1. *Life Connection*
- Have you or has someone you know been anointed with oil for healing, physical or emotional? Record that instance below. _____

_____

_____

_____

2. *Content Questions*
- What were some general uses of oil in ancient times? _____

_____

_____

_____

- Look up the following examples of anointing with oil in the Old Testament. Comment on the meaning of the anointing in each case.
1 Samuel 16:6 _____

_____

1 Samuel 24:6, 10 _____

_____

2 Samuel 23:1 _____

_____

Psalm 2:2 _____

_____

- Who is God's anointed one in the New Testament era (Acts 4:26, 27)?

_____

_____

- Use your own words to describe Jesus' calling as the anointed one. What has he come to heal? _____

  _____

  _____

- Read James 5:13. Who is the healer referred to in this passage?

  _____

  _____

- How does each of the following passages refer to an anointing that results in empowerment?
  2 Corinthians 1:21–22 _____

  _____

  1 John 2:20 _____

  _____

- Describe the anointing that takes place in a worship service today.

  _____

  _____

  _____

  _____

- Describe the anointing that takes place in a hospital today.

  _____

  _____

  _____

  _____

- What sacred action takes place at the anointing?

  _____

  _____

  _____

3. *Application*

- Pray the prayer of anointing in the text. Reflect on its simplicity and profound meaning. Would you like to have someone pray for you for a physical illness, emotional stress, or empowerment in life?

PART II: GROUP DISCUSSION

The following questions are designed for group discussion. Share the insights you gained from your personal study in Part I.

Write out all answers that group members give to the questions on a chalkboard, a flip chart, or a dry erase board.

1. *Life Connection*
   - Begin your discussion by asking persons in the group to relate stories of family or friends who have received the anointing of oil.

2. *Thought Questions*
   - In general, how has oil been used in ancient times and today? What do these uses of oil say about the symbolic meaning of oil?
   - Study the biblical references to anointing with oil (1 Sam 16:6; 24:6, 10; 2 Sam 23:1; Ps 2:2). What does each say about the symbolism of oil?
   - Jesus is called the anointed one (Acts 4:26–27). Discuss the healing Jesus has come to accomplish. Why is the healing done by the church always in the name of Jesus?
   - How would you describe the anointing known as empowerment?

3. *Application*
   - Evaluate the healing ministry of your church. Is it done exclusively through counseling? Or are there ministers for the laying on of hands with oil?
   - Take time in class to do the ministry of healing. Ask if anyone would like to be prayed for (the leader may volunteer first). Follow the guidelines set forth in the text.
   - What have you learned about God in this session? About yourself?

ASHES TO ASHES

A Study in Funeral Rites

A colleague of mine at Wheaton College, a man deeply committed to worship renewal, recently died of cancer. He lived for less than a year after the stunning diagnosis. For him that was an important year. He told people, "I thank God I have some time to reflect on my death and the meaning of my life."

During that time he prepared his funeral. Like his life, his funeral was a celebration. If was a fourfold pattern of worship with the eucharist. The Communion songs focused on the resurrection. There were tears, of course. But it was a bright sadness. It was a funeral service full of the sounds of hope and continuing life.

I thought of his funeral service in contrast to so many other funerals I have attended in my lifetime. Many of those funerals, which were characterized by the mournful sounds of death and wailing, focused on death rather than the hope that is ours because of the resurrection.

In worship renewal, the funeral service is shifted from the sounds of death to the new sound of hope and joy. Let's look at this ritual more carefully.

THE BIBLICAL BACKGROUND

The Scriptures do not give a great deal of information about burial rites. Most of what we know surrounds the burial of Jesus.

Generally the body was bathed with oil before it was wrapped for burial. Jesus' body was not bathed in oil because of his hasty burial (no burials on the Sabbath). But the gospels do record that his body was wrapped in linens with myrrh and aloe between the bands. He was then laid to rest in the tomb (see Matt 27:59–60; Mark 15:46; Luke 23:53, 56; John 19:38–40).

Jewish tradition viewed dead bodies as unclean. Consequently, they were buried before people went back to work or said their prayers. The mournful side of death was demonstrated in the rules for the family: they were forbidden to work, to bathe, or to have sexual intercourse for up to thirty days. The men were served a "cold comfort" meal after the funeral. This meal consisted of eggs and lentils prepared by neighbors. For a period of eleven months following the death of a parent, the children were to recite the Kaddish, a prayer similar to the Lord's Prayer, every day.

EARLY CHRISTIAN RITUALS

We do not have a great deal of information about funeral rites in the early church. What we do know comes from inscriptions in the burial places within the catacombs. These inscriptions emphasize the deliverance that came through Jesus. Consequently, predominate symbols include the raising of Lazarus and other miracles of Jesus. There are also records of meals held after the burial.

The oldest actual record of burial practice comes from the seventh century. It consists of two parts: sacred actions in the home as the person was dying, and sacred actions at the grave site.

In the home the Christian was given the eucharist as an expression of both the death of Christ and the resurrection that the dying Christian would soon experience. Then family and friends read the passion narrative to the dying family member. As death approached, those gathered would say, "Come saints of God, advance angels of the Lord." Then they recited Psalm 113 together and concluded by praying, "May the choir of angels receive you."

After the person died, the body was placed on boards and carried in a procession to the church. The community then held a simple service of prayers and psalms. The antiphon used was "may the angels lead you into paradise, may the martyrs welcome you and guide you into the holy city Jerusalem." Then as they recited Psalm 117, they took the body to the cemetery for burial. There they recited the antiphon "open the gates for me, and once I am within I shall praise the Lord."

FUNERAL RITES TODAY

Funeral rites have gone through some significant changes since the early church. In the medieval era funerals emphasized the judgment and purgatory, yet with the hope of new life. The Reformers emphasized the resurrection in their funeral rites, but gradually many Protestant funerals shifted toward a mournful experience coupled with words of hope.

Today in worship renewal, the funeral is more like the celebration I described in the opening paragraphs. The funeral is now a *full service of worship* and normally held in the church rather than in a funeral home. The funeral in the church is in itself an expression of the spiritual nature of the ritual. The full service of worship shows it to be an act of worship. In worship we join with the heavenly host—the angels, the archangels, the cherubim, the seraphim, and the whole company of saints—who gather around the throne to sing the new song (see Rev 5:11–14). This view of worship, which is rooted in the communion of saints, affirms that when we worship, we worship together with those who are dead but now alive with Christ in the heavens. Consequently, a funeral rite is properly a ritual done within the context of worship.

Conclusion

I want to close with a personal comment about the view of the funeral in worship renewal. This idea that we worship together with the saints is a matter of great comfort to those who have lost loved ones. My mother and father are both dead, but when I am in worship, I am together with them at God's throne. While I do not think of this truth continuously, when I do it gives me comfort and hope. So make sure that funerals in your church are testimonies to the resurrection.

STUDY GUIDE

Read Session 11, "Ashes to Ashes,"
before starting the study guide.

PART I: PERSONAL STUDY

Complete the following questions individually.

1. *Life Connection*
- Reflect on funerals you have attended. Were they filled with sadness and dread? Record your memories below.

_____

_____

_____

_____

2. *Content Questions*
- Read John 19:38–42 and describe the rituals of Jewish burial.

_____

_____

_____

_____

- Briefly summarize in your own words the Jewish rules and regulations surrounding death.

_____

_____

_____

_____

- What do we know about death and funerals in the early church?

_____

_____

_____

_____

- Summarize the two parts of the funeral service that developed after the seventh century. _____

  _____

  _____

  _____

  _____

- Read Psalm 113. What portions of this Scripture would be especially comforting to a dying person? _____

  _____

  _____

  _____

- Read Psalm 117. How would this psalm speak to the grieving family?

  _____

  _____

  _____

  _____

- Describe the funeral rites of today. Emphasize changes that have resulted from worship renewal. _____

  _____

  _____

  _____

  _____

3. *Application*

- Briefly describe the kind of funeral you want for yourself. _____

  _____

  _____

  _____

  _____

  _____

  _____

PART II: GROUP DISCUSSION

The following questions are designed for group discussion. Share the insights you gained from your personal study in Part I.

Write out all answers that group members give to the questions on a chalkboard, a flip chart, or a dry erase board.

1. *Life Connection*
   ◆ Begin your discussion by asking members of the group to describe funerals they have attended recently. Were they mournful or joyful?

2. *Thought Questions*
   ◆ Read John 19:38–42. Discuss the burial of Jesus as an example of burial rites in the Jewish tradition. What rituals helped them face death?
   ◆ How do you think the Jewish rules and regulations surrounding death helped the family cope with death? Would you wish for similar rituals today?
   ◆ Why should the approach to a funeral be oriented toward the resurrection, as it was in the early church?
   ◆ What elements of seventh-century funeral rites would you want in a funeral today?
   ◆ Read the following psalms and comment on their message:

   Psalm 113   Read to the dying
   Psalm 117   Read for the family

   ◆ How have funerals changed as a result of twentieth-century worship renewal?

3. *Application*
   ◆ Obtain the funeral rite of your church. Read through it, commenting on the meaning of the words and phrases. Read the recommended Scriptures. Is this a mournful ritual or one that emphasizes the resurrection and hope?

- If your church does not have a prescribed funeral rite, take some time to prepare one. You may want to borrow a ritual from another tradition to serve as a guide.
- Ask each person to plan his or her own funeral. Ask several people to present their suggested funeral services.

PART III

~∾∾∾~

OTHER SACRED

ACTIONS OF

WORSHIP

HUMBLE YOURSELF

A *Study in Foot Washing*

A number of years ago I was involved in a community known as the Church of the Brethren. The Church of the Brethren is a branch of the Anabaptist community, a group of believers who trace their modern beginnings back to the sixteenth century.

The Anabaptists include the Amish, the Hutterites, the Mennonites, as well as the Church of the Brethren. A major emphasis of the Anabaptists is their commitment to a simple life and the spreading of God's peace in personal, familial, and national relationships.

A sacred action that stands at the heart of the Anabaptist community is the washing of feet. This action occurs in the larger context of the agape feast, which is celebrated from one to three times a year, depending on the church and its traditions.

This worship occasion includes three parts: the agape feast (a full meal), the washing of feet, and the breaking of bread.

At the time I experienced the washing of the feet in the Church of the Brethren, I was unaware that liturgical churches also practice the washing of feet once a year at the Maundy Thursday service. Let's look at this sacred action more closely and seek to understand how we may use it in our worship.

THE BIBLICAL BASIS

The origins of foot washing lie in the ancient Middle Eastern custom of hospitality. Guests to a home may have walked for miles through dusty roads and paths, arriving with their feet dirty and, in some cases, caked from travel. Foot bathing basins were available for guests upon arrival. Either the host or the servants of the host would wash the guest's feet as a sign of hospitality (see 1 Sam 25:41).

There are three examples of foot washing in the New Testament. The first is the story of a woman who washed Jesus' feet (Luke 7:36–38; apparently the host was inhospitable to Jesus). The second is simply a reference to foot washing as the demonstration of good character (1 Tim 5:9–10). The third and most important is the example of Jesus' washing the feet of his disciples (John 13:1–20).

The occasion in which Jesus washed the feet of his disciples was, of course, a very significant one for Jesus. It was the night before his death. The point he wanted to make is stated in verses 15 and 16: "I have set you an example that you should do as I have done for you. I tell you the truth, no servant is greater than his master, nor is a messenger greater than the one who sent him" (John 13:15–16).

INTERPRETATION OF FOOT WASHING

The founding text of foot washing (John 13:1–20) contains two different interpretations of footwashing: the need for regular spiritual cleansing and the admonition to be humble.

The first, the need for regular spiritual cleansing, is based on the interpretation of verses 6–10. When Peter resisted having his feet washed, Jesus said, "Unless I wash you, you have no part with me" (v. 8). Then Jesus concluded the dialogue with Peter by saying, "A person who has had a bath needs only to wash his feet; his whole body is clean. And you are clean, though not every one of you" (v. 10). That final phrase "though not every one of you" refers, as the next verse shows, to Judas. But Jesus had obviously washed his feet. So the reference must have to do with not just the outward cleansing of the feet but with the inner cleansing of the heart. Judas' feet were clean, but his heart was full of betrayal.

The second interpretation is based on verses 14–17 which teach that Jesus is leaving them with an example of self-sacrificial humility. The message is clear that God's servants are not to demand service from others (or themselves), but like Jesus they are called to lead lives of service to others.

It is this latter message that has given shape to the Anabaptist view of life. They do not clamor after riches, fame, or power. Instead they are empowered by this central image of Jesus who gives his life in self-sacrificing servanthood. This concept of servanthood has been the motivating factor in the Anabaptist community, more so than in the Catholic and general Protestant communities, which have tended to emphasize correct doctrine.

Foot Washing Today

The practice of foot washing has never enjoyed universal acceptance in the church and is not likely to attain it in the twenty-first century.

Anabaptists will continue the practice. However, some Anabaptist churches, because of the influx of persons from other Protestant communities, are beginning to lose their distinctiveness. With that, the practice of foot washing is going into decline.

On the other hand, the recovery of the Christian year among Protestants has brought with it a new interest in the worship practices of the ancient church. Consequently, there is more foot washing among Protestants in the Maundy Thursday service. This service, like the love feast of the Anabaptist communities, consists of three parts: an agape feast, foot washing, and the institution of the Lord's Supper.

We can hope that churches recovering the foot washing on Maundy Thursday will find ways to make this sacred action more lavish so that it communicates the meaning of self-sacrificial service.

Conclusion

We live in a "get-all-you-can" world where many people think only of themselves and their families. The selfish lifestyle has also affected the Christian world, which needs a new infusion of humility and a desire to serve others. The recovery of foot washing may do just that in our churches, turning us away from ourselves to serve others.

Read Session 12, "Humble Yourself,"
before starting the study guide.

PART I: PERSONAL STUDY

Complete the following questions individually.

1. *Life Connection*

- Have you experienced foot washing in a worship setting, either in an Anabaptist church or in the Maundy Thursday service of the liturgical church? Describe your experience, including your feelings. _____

  _____

  _____

  _____

  _____

2. *Content Questions*

- Describe the origins of the washing of feet in the ancient culture of the Middle East._____

  _____

  _____

  _____

  _____

- Read Luke 7:36–38. What is the point of the foot washing in this setting?

  _____

  _____

  _____

  _____

- Read 1 Timothy 5:9–10. What is the point of foot washing in this setting?

  _____

  _____

  _____

- Read John 13:1–20. What was the point Jesus made by the washing of feet? _____

_____

_____

_____

- What two interpretations are given to the John 13:1–20 incident?
  a. _____

  _____

  b. _____

  _____

- How is the need of spiritual cleansing drawn from John 13:6–10?

  _____

  _____

  _____

  _____

- How is the need for humility drawn from John 13:14–17? _____

  _____

  _____

  _____

  _____

- How has the emphasis on humility shaped the Anabaptist view of life?

  _____

  _____

  _____

  _____

- Why is foot washing practiced on Maundy Thursday?

  _____

  _____

  _____

  _____

3. *Application*

♦ If you have never experienced the spiritual event of foot washing, think of a context in which it might occur. Can you make it happen? Whose feet would you want to wash? _____

_____

_____

_____

PART II: GROUP DISCUSSION

The following questions are designed for group discussion. Share the insights you gained from your personal study in Part I.

Write out all answers that group members give to the questions on a chalkboard, a flip chart, or a dry erase board.

1. *Life Connection*

♦ Begin class discussion by asking people to relate their experience of foot washing within the context of worship. How did they feel about the experience?

2. *Thought Questions*

♦ Talk about the experience of foot washing in the ancient Middle East. Imagine the custom of washing the feet of those who have journeyed on dusty roads. Would you wash the feet of your guest or would you have a servant do it?

♦ Read the following Scriptures and discuss the point of foot washing in each.

　　Luke 7:36–38
　　1 Timothy 5:9–10
　　John 13:1–20

♦ Discuss the two interpretations of John 13:1–20. Explain the argument for each interpretation. Which do you prefer?

♦ How has foot washing affected the Anabaptist community? Give examples.

3. *Application*

- Evaluate the use of foot washing in your church. Do you regard foot washing to be a command by Jesus to be continued in the church? Or do you think the John 13:1–20 passage is limited to the culture of the New Testament?

- Should your church develop the custom of a yearly feast with foot washing and Communion? Would you do this on Maundy Thursday or at another time? Would everyone wash feet or only a few, for symbolic purposes?

RETURN TO THE LORD

A Study in the Solemn Assembly

 I have always known about the Old Testament solemn assembly and the renewals of Israel that happened in relationship to them. But I wasn't aware until a few years ago that the solemn assembly was being practiced today in a local church as a means of renewing the church.

I met with some church leaders in Nashville who were talking of the tremendous renewing results of the solemn assembly in various churches. My curiosity piqued, I asked, "Where can I go to experience the solemn assembly?" A church in the Dallas area was holding one soon, so I quickly made arrangements and went.

It was, as they had promised, "a real experience." I wasn't able to stay for the entire time because of a previous engagement, but the experience consisted of an intense three-day (weekend) time of spiritual inquiry, repentance, reconciliation, and renewal.

THE BIBLICAL BASIS

A biblical solemn assembly may be defined as a period of time in which God's people come together to confess their sins and to come into a renewed relationship with God.

The spirit of this convocation is captured by 2 Chronicles 7:14: "If my people, who are called by my name, will humble themselves and pray and seek my face and turn from their wicked ways, then I will hear from heaven and will forgive their sin and will heal their land."

The Old Testament records many solemn assemblies:
- Exodus 33:7–11
- 1 Samuel 7:5–6
- 2 Samuel 6:14–19 (1 Chron 13:1–8)
- 2 Chronicles 15:9–15

- 2 Chronicles 29:5–29
- 2 Chronicles 34:31–33
- Ezra 6:16–22
- Ezra 8:21–23; 9:5–15; 10:7–12
- Nehemiah 8:1–12
- Joel 1:14; 2:12–17, 19, 28–29

All of these solemn assemblies have four characteristics in common.
- Israel was in a state of rebellion against God.
- God had sent a form of judgment upon the people.
- The leaders of Israel became aware of their situation, saw the judgment coming, and recognized the judgment as a result of Israel's sin.
- The leaders took action to bring Israel to repentance and renewal. They responded to God's call for a solemn assembly.

THE SOLEMN ASSEMBLY TODAY

There are no records of a solemn assembly in the New Testament. This may be because God dealt with the nation of Israel, but the church is scattered among the nations of the world.

There is, however, a kind of solemn assembly *time* in the Christian church—Lent. During Lent the church universal is called upon to spend time reflecting on individual and corporate sin, to carry that sin into the tomb with Christ, and to be raised to new life in Christ in the resurrection.

Today some are calling for solemn assemblies in the local church and/or a national solemn assembly because of the sins of the American people.

Most of the leadership for a national solemn assembly has come from the Southern Baptist Church. Their motivation in seeking such an assembly, according to P. Preston Graham, a Southern Baptist leader, is based in the following convictions:
- God is holy and hates sin.
- America has turned away from God.
- America has become a very sinful nation.
- God has begun America's judgment.
- The judgment is currently remedial in nature.
- If repentance does not occur, the judgment will be final.
- The only hope America has is prayer and revival.

* National revival is needed.
* Extraordinary commitment to prayer is needed.

CONCLUSION

Throughout the history of Israel and again throughout the history of the church, God's people have fallen away from the truth and into rebellion against God.

There is value for us in reflecting on the sacred action of the solemn assembly, God's way of dealing with Israel. And we may ask, Could this ancient way of dealing with sin be effective in the life of the local church, the universal church, and the nation? It is a complicated question, but one worth addressing.

STUDY GUIDE

Read Session 13, "Return to the Lord,"
before starting the study guide.

PART I: PERSONAL STUDY

Complete the following questions individually.

1. *Life Connection*
- Have you been involved in a solemn assembly or in any retreat that had spiritual renewal as the goal? What happened? _____
  _____
  _____
  _____
  _____

2. *Content Questions*
- Define the solemn assembly. _____
  _____
  _____
  _____
  _____

- What is the message of 2 Chronicles 7:14? _____
  _____
  _____
  _____
  _____

- What are the four themes common to the solemn assemblies of the Old Testament?
  a. _____
  b. _____
  c. _____
  d. _____

- Read 2 Chronicles 29:5–29 and identify all four steps of the solemn assembly. List the passages below and summarize the action.
  a. _____

  _____
  b. _____

  _____
  c. _____

  _____
  d. _____

  _____

- How may the Lenten season function as a solemn assembly of the Old Testament? _____

  _____

  _____

  _____

  _____

- Use your own words to summarize the seven motivating factors for a solemn assembly today.
  a. _____
  b. _____
  c. _____
  d. _____
  e. _____
  f. _____
  g. _____

3. *Application*

- How would a solemn assembly be received in your church today?

  _____

  _____

  _____

  _____

  _____

PART II: GROUP DISCUSSION

The following questions are designed for group discussion. Share the insights you gained from your personal study in Part I.

> Write out all answers that group members give to the questions on a chalkboard, a flip chart, or a dry erase board.

1. *Life Connection*
   - Begin your discussion by asking members of the class to relate their experience in a solemn assembly or in any similar retreat geared toward repentance and renewal.

2. *Thought Questions*
   - How is a solemn assembly defined?
   - Read 2 Chronicles 7:14. Is this message only for Israel, or does it apply to groups of people and even nations today?
   - Review the four themes common to Old Testament solemn assemblies.
   - Read 2 Chronicles 29:5–29. Identify the four steps of the solemn assembly in this passage.
   - Review the seven motivating factors for the solemn assembly today.

3. *Application*
   - Do you think the Lenten season could be used to initiate a solemn assembly? Would you want one in your church?
   - Brainstorm the content of the solemn assembly for your church. How would you organize it? What would you do?